YOU RAISED ME UP

June Mascarenhas

First published 2022
by Rowanvale Books Ltd
The Gate
Keppoch Street
Roath
Cardiff
CF24 3JW
www.rowanvalebooks.com

A CIP catalogue record for this book is available from
the British Library.
ISBN: 978-1-913662-85-1

This is a work of fiction. Names, characters, businesses, places, events and incidents are either the products of the author's imagination or used in a fictitious manner. Any resemblance to actual persons, living or dead, or actual events is purely coincidental.

DAN, you are my world

"To belittle you have to be little." - Khalil Gibran

"Blowing out my candle will not make yours glow any brighter." - Nigerian Proverb

CHAPTER 1

"THE WORLD'S GREATEST"

January 2005

Laila had lost count of the number of times she woke up praying that her mother would die. Today was no different.

She was staring at the ceiling when the shrill ringing of the phone by her bedside startled her. It was 5:55 a.m. Who could be calling so early? Instinct told her it could only be bad news. She could feel it in every fibre of her being.

Laila grabbed the phone, but Lalita, her fourteen-year-old daughter, had already picked up the extension in the kitchen. It was Thursday. Her girls would be eating their cereal at that ridiculous round granite table. It could seat twelve people easily! What had possessed the previous manager to order such a large table?

"Is your mama awake, Lalita?" Tamer's voice seemed to come from miles away. Of course, Bath was not round the corner from Sharm El Sheikh, but there were times when the line was so clear she would think Tamer was calling from the next room. Today was not one of those days.

Laila cut in before Lalita could reply. "I've got it, Lali."

1

The familiar click didn't sound. Laila knew Lalita hadn't hung up. Kindred spirits; her youngest daughter had sensed bad news as well.

Laila listened to soft sobbing. Tamer's sorrow flowed down the telephone line. Tangible, even with the bad connection. This was going to be a difficult conversation.

"Is it Mummy?" Laila asked.

The sobs came and went. Damn the line.

"Tamer, get a grip. Tell me, what is it?"

She knew what was coming; putting it into words would make it real. Believable.

"Mum. Mum died this morning at five-thirty a.m. I want to die too. She's gone. She's gone." Tamer's voice faded.

Thank you, Lord, Laila thought. Her mother was in safe hands now.

Immediately, guilt engulfed her. Should she really be thanking God? How could she? She was the worst daughter. No daughter should feel like this on hearing of her mother's death. But she couldn't deny the feeling of relief that washed over her.

Five years of suffering for her mother had finally come to an end. The disease had left a gregarious woman a mere shadow of herself. Unable to move, articulate herself or eat. Food had been her mother's passion. Any food, whether Indian, Italian or Iranian, she ate with gusto, relishing every bite. For nearly a year, her food had needed to be pureed to reduce choking. Crab curries and pork spareribs had been replaced with mashed potatoes and vegetable soups. Meals that Lakshmi swallowed without tasting.

When Lakshmi could no longer take the stairs, her bed had been moved down to the dining room. Laila shuddered, remembering how the cockroaches had scuttled from her mother's face when she had put on the dining room light. She had stepped on them savagely, putting all her anger into the task. Lakshmi had lain rigid on the bed, unable to brush them away, her eyes wide, brimming with unshed tears. Laila had wanted to scream her frustration. How could this be happening to her mother?

The glass of water she had come down for had been forgotten, her thirst replaced by fury, frustration and misery.

"Why, Mummy, is God testing you so dearly?" Laila had whispered as she held her mother's hand.

Was this empty life her mother was living worth it? Laila had sat by her mother's bedside and cried. Powerless.

With stiff fingers, Lakshmi had brushed her tears away until Laila had fallen asleep on her mother's chest.

PSP. A small name for a dreadful disease that had deprived her mother of movement. Progressive Supranuclear Palsy, the neurosurgeon had explained, was rare. Not that rare, Laila had thought at that time. It had found her mother. Her wonderful, beautiful, intelligent mother, Lakshmi. A name indeed fit for a goddess. The goddess had become a blurred figment of imagination once the disease had ravaged her body and mind.

The vibrant woman whom Laila had argued with while growing up, the woman she had come to love with all her heart when she married and had children of her own, had receded further and further into a dark, dusty corner of an attic that was no longer visited. The disease had stripped her of all movement, speech and articulation. Not all at once, but painfully over the five years. Like a drip in the arm of a patient,

3

drop by drop, until she was unrecognisable even to her own family. The last year had been the hardest. The once plump Lakshmi became as thin and brittle as a twig. The flesh around her stomach and her behind hung in wrinkly folds like a hundred-year-old pachyderm.

"I bought you diet pills," Laila had told her once, before the disease. "Green tea and black radish. It claims to shed weight in record time if taken on an empty stomach. Why don't you give it a try, Mummy?"

"Are you saying I'm fat?" Lakshmi had demanded, before letting out one of her loud, infectious laughs.

"Not exactly fat, just in need of shedding one or two kilos," Laila said in her most cajoling voice.

"You don't fool me, Laila Cardoso. I know you think me fat." Lakshmi was not to be outdone. "For your information, young lady, I happen to like my voluptuous figure." She ran her hands sexily down her body.

"Please just give them a try. Please." Laila tried to be persuasive, proffering the dark brown jar.

Lakshmi turned it around and read the label.

"Big promises from such a little bottle. Fine, Laila my child, I'll give it a try, for you."

"Thanks, Ma!" Laila smiled sheepishly.

The pleas, rants and humour had fallen on deaf ears. Lakshmi would start a diet but give up. Good intentions of exercising would be cast aside with excuses of housework and weather conditions within days.

The extra kilos had been a godsend when Lakshmi had melted like butter on a hot pavement. Eyes seeing and brain comprehending. Unlike other neurological illnesses where the patient is often oblivious, with PSP, the mind continued to work perfectly. Lakshmi's inability to voice her distress and horror at how she had metamorphosed was heart-breaking, not only for her but for the family.

The transition from panties to Pampers had left Lakshmi not only helpless but embarrassed and distraught. She'd refused to make eye contact for weeks, her lower lip trembling when it was time for a change.

"Laila, can you get onto the next available flight?" Tamer's voice jolted Laila back to the present. She would, as usual, be the one handling things. The thought wouldn't even have crossed Tamer's mind that he could be the one to go. Lakshmi had spoilt him, like any Indian mother. He was used to getting his way.

She wouldn't argue about it though. Not now. "I'll have a look at what flights leave for Nairobi. When will you leave?"

"I don't know, I'll have to check. Can you handle the funeral arrangements?"

"*What else?*" Laila wanted to snap, but today was not the day. Laila swallowed her resentment. She murmured that she would see Tamer soon, resisting the urge to slam the receiver down.

Family had meant everything to Lakshmi. She had urged them to be close-knit, to stand together and not to let misunderstandings and sibling rivalry stand in the way of unity and love. *Forgive and forget* was her favourite motto.

"Don't wash your dirty laundry in public." Laila could hear Lakshmi admonishing her.

Lalita and Lili, Laila's eldest daughter, entered the bedroom with Kurt, their father, in tow. Their cheeks were damp with tears. Laila knew that no words would lessen the sense of loss. Kurt took Laila's

5

hand in his, sitting beside her on the bed. His sobs were uncontrollable. Laila sighed. She squeezed Kurt's hand and hugged him. She would have to do the comforting instead of being comforted.

Her husband and her mother had held a special relationship. They'd adored each other, a rarity.

She listened for a while to the sound of the three people she loved engulfed in sorrow, tears streaking their cheeks, and wondered when her own tears would come. Not now. They needed her, she had to be strong. She prided herself on being an oak, although she felt like a weeping willow today.

Pulling away from Kurt's embrace, Laila stood. The bedroom was still in darkness. She walked over to the window and drew back the blackout curtains.

Majestic palm trees swayed in the cool morning breeze. The pink and blue sky was coming awake. Tiny clouds scattered in the distance like sheep rounded up by a collie. The Red Sea shone in the dawn light, a cobalt blue, and the lush green grass sparkled like diamonds after the last night's rain. The lawns were magnificently tended by the hotel gardeners.

It was beautiful in the resort town of Sharm El Sheikh. Laila never took for granted the view that greeted her every morning. She was lucky to be living in this picture-postcard world with bougainvillea and herbaceous hedges in every conceivable colour lining the walkways. In the distance, she could see the private marina. The luxurious yacht that docked there for most of the year was been hosed down by the skipper. It belonged to one of the princes of Saudi Arabia.

"Can you ask your assistant to book my ticket, Kurt?" Laila didn't turn around. She wanted to take in the beauty in front of her. "If I could leave as soon as possible. I have to help my father with the funeral arrangements. He won't cope alone."

Laila was a woman of few words. Short sentences were her forte.

"Of course I will. Why don't you come down for breakfast? You have to eat." Kurt stood close behind Laila without touching her. His tall, broad-shouldered shadow fell across her petite frame. Laila could smell the minty toothpaste on his breath.

Laila nodded and followed Kurt down the stairs. She knew the food would be like walnut kernels in her mouth.

Why hadn't she called home yesterday? A crow had squawked outside the dining room the entire afternoon. She had known it was a bad omen. Didn't crows and death go hand in hand? She had shooed it away a couple of times, but it had persistently perched back on the rattan table. Caw! Caw! Shrill. Insistent. A doom bearer.

Laila knew why she hadn't made the call. She couldn't bear to hear her mother grunt down the phone when she asked how she was. Lakshmi was forever fine, never one to complain. It was even worse when she tried to formulate 'I love you' with grunts and rasps.

Regret tore at her. Not having spoken one last time with her mother would haunt her forever. Even a grunt would be welcome today. She would never again hear her mother struggle to speak. Death had taken care of that.

The finality of death only dawns when one loses a loved one.

"Mama? I'm so sorry about Nan." Lalita stood beside Laila, slightly brushing the tips of her mother's fingers.

"I know, baby. I'll be okay. You and Lili don't need to go to school today." Laila moved to stand by the kitchen window. She had torn the fluffy croissant in half, but today it wasn't appealing and lay untouched.

From where she stood, Laila could see the entrance of the hotel. The security guard lifted the boom to let a Kuoni minivan enter with tourists admiring their surroundings, taking photographs and videos. Chatting loudly in German, excited to get their vacation started. They would be sprawled on the silver sands in a while, turning the colour of lobsters in a couple of days. Some would even need medical attention due to severe burns.

"We have exams, we have to go," Lalita said. "Will you be here when we get back?"

"I don't know." Laila shrugged. "It depends what flights are available. I'll call you if I have to leave earlier. Where's Lili?"

"In the sitting room, I think."

"I don't know how long I'll be gone, Lali. You and your sis have to take care of things."

Living in the hotel had its perks. As daughters of the general manager, the girls wouldn't have to bother about cooking or cleaning.

Laila caught Kurt and Lili hastily brushing away their tears as she entered the sitting room.

Laila stood behind Lili, stroking her hair. "I may be gone for several weeks. Don't trouble your father, and study hard." As an afterthought, she added, "Don't cry, Lili. Your nan wouldn't want it. She's happy. Probably dancing in heaven now that she can, without the shackles around her body restraining her every move. She must be walking on sunshine."

"I loved her so much. I can't believe she's gone." Lili choked on a sob. She brushed her long, chestnut hair away from her face.

A few months ago, she had insisted on travelling to Nairobi to see Lakshmi. Laila had been apprehensive of how her sensitive daughter would react to seeing her happy-go-lucky grandmother so transformed. Lili had surprised her with her staunchness and courage. She had been gentle and affectionate, showering Lakshmi with hugs and kisses. She had read to her grandmother and combed her hair. Sang her "Downtown" by Petula Clark, "Sway" by Dean Martin, "Blueberry Hill" by Fats Domino and "Your Cheating Heart" by Patsy Cline. Some of Lakshmi's favourite songs.

"And she loved you, Lili; always remember that. You were her first grandchild."

Once the girls left on the school bus, Laila threw herself into what needed to get done. Starting with packing. She would need black outfits, something her wardrobe lacked, she realised after rummaging. She would have to make do with black trousers and her LBD. Once the packing was out of the way, she started on the list for Lili and Lalita. Kurt's list was longer, detailing what the girls liked to eat, which day was laundry, homework, after school activities and weekend curfew.

Kurt called to say that an open return ticket had been purchased. Laila sighed. She had done that often today; she sounded like Lakshmi.

Nairobi was her home, and she loved going back, but having to stay indefinitely was daunting. Water and electricity shortages were a thing of the past for her. Dusty roads and tedious traffic jams of two, three, or even more hours didn't bear thinking about.

Her childhood home was tiny compared to the spacious villa in Sharm El Sheikh. Four en-suite bedrooms with white gleaming marble floors and wide balconies were luxuries they couldn't have afforded. Housekeeping on a daily basis and room service whenever Laila didn't feel like whipping up a meal. A chauffeur-driven Range Rover, eating in the hotel's Iranian and Italian fine-dining restaurants, body scrubs and massages, sauna and steam baths.

The school bus arrived just as Laila and Kurt were leaving for the airport. Laila hugged her daughters tightly.

"I love you very much. Be good. I'll Skype you every day if the internet works." She made a face. Internet connectivity was haphazard in Kenya.

After check-in, Laila slumped down on the metal seat. The enormity of why she was going to Nairobi dawned on her. Her mother was gone. She would never see her again. Hold her hand or talk to her, even though it had been one-sided for many months. Laila had become good at decoding the guttural sounds and slurred speech that had become Lakshmi's way of communicating.

In her heyday, Lakshmi had been an eloquent speaker. She could make a story come alive with expressions and intonations. A pocket dictionary was one of many items to be found in her handbag, so she could look up unfamiliar words and know how to spell them. Laila remembered how, years ago, her mother had asked her to spell 'bougainvillea'. She had mixed up the ending. Lakshmi had made her write down the word ten times. Weekends were spent having spelling-bee competitions when Tamer and Laila were growing up, their mother the strict umpire. Lakshmi was unbeatable at Scrabble.

She was miles ahead of her friends and relatives in savoir faire and intelligence. She was the soul at every party or gathering. She could sing and dance; the waltz had been her favourite. She was an excellent cook, willingly giving recipes without keeping key ingredients to herself like many of her friends. Mangoes were distributed to everyone in the neighbourhood when the trees in the back yard were heaving with fruit from November. Neighbours in the same street let guavas, avocadoes, papayas and bananas rot rather than distribute them.

"Are you ladies talking about Sheila again?" Laila had watched as Lakshmi confronted the four neighbourhood ladies—back in the days when she worked. "Don't you women have anything better to do? There's no need for idle tittle-tattle."

She'd stood on the dusty pavement until they'd all gone back inside. Lakshmi never minced her words. She was an avid defender of the down-trodden.

Then, her prayer group had stopped inviting her to the Wednesday gatherings at the early stages of PSP. Laila had wondered at their unkindness when Lakshmi needed them the most.

"What's wrong with Lakshmi?" they'd whispered among themselves. "Is it depression? She seems odd and not all there."

Why couldn't they have directed their questions to Lakshmi or Amit instead of talking about her? It had riled Laila, who had wanted to confront their cowardice.

Lakshmi had been adamant, shaking her head fiercely. "They have already made up their minds that I am slowly going mad, Laila. Let it be. I don't need to explain my illness to them."

Her mother had been in a league of her own.

Soft tears turned into uncontrollable sobs. Laila felt like she was being held underwater, drowning. The tears wouldn't stop. Panic engulfed her. How would she go through life without her mother? Who would be there to guide her? To advise her? To assuage all her fears? *Yes, Lord, I prayed for my mother's death, never knowing that the emptiness would be all encompassing, stifling.* No matter her illness, the loss was overwhelming. Final. Would it be like a scar that never fades?

"Are you okay?"

Laila lifted her heavy head with effort to find an elderly man in front of her. His cream gallabiyah was creased and could do with a wash.

"Are you okay?" he repeated, his grey eyebrows slightly frowning.

"I'm fine." Laila dabbed at her eyes. She had been sobbing audibly. "Thank you."

"Today's sorrow will pass." He fleetingly touched Laila's right shoulder before shuffling away.

Would it, though? Her determination had stopped her from breaking down in front of her family. She regretted it now. She'd have done anything to have Kurt's strong arms around her or hugs and kisses from her daughters. Laila knew she was like her father in that aspect. Reserved. Staunch. Why hadn't she kissed Lakshmi more often or told her that she meant the world to her? That she loved her?

It was too late for regrets. "Life is short" only made sense once you lost someone you loved. Couldn't death be like a return policy? If you didn't like what life had meted out, you could ask to go back. Change a few things. Live differently. Demand a refund.

The flight was practically empty, and the three vacant seats were welcome neighbours. Laila stretched out. She dozed on and off and cried on and off. Just three weeks ago, she'd been on this same flight going to celebrate her mother's seventieth birthday. Before saying goodbye, Lakshmi had struggled to put into words that it would be the last time that Laila would see her. She had insisted that she wanted to be cremated. Laila even managed to grasp what flowers she wanted. With extreme effort, she had rasped out, "I love you, Laila, very much." After she had given her blessings, she had added, "I'm so proud of you." Laila had sobbed on her mother's lap. Cursing the disease. Wishing for her mother's release from the illness.

Do we know when our time has come? Laila wondered. *Do we get a sign from above?*

The man who met Laila at arrivals at Jomo Kenyatta International Airport couldn't have been her father. Amit was a mirage of the man he'd been three weeks ago. His shoulders were stooped, his face sallow and waxy.

His partner of fifty years was no more. Lakshmi had been the backbone of the Cardoso family. Even her illness had been unable to take away the strength she commanded in the house. It had been less than twenty-four hours and already her loss was as encompassing and indelible as an ink stain on a blotter, getting larger.

Would they ever be the same?

Laila wrapped her arms around her father, at a loss for words. Sorry seemed too small. It didn't quite portray all that she wanted to say.

"Were you by Mummy's side when she died?" Laila needed to know.

"No, Laila, I came down and she had already gone. It couldn't have been long. She was still warm."

Her mother had died alone.

Laila cursed fate, choking back her anger at the unfairness of life. Lakshmi would have loved her hand to be held on her way toward the light.

The house was different. Empty.

The bed against the dining room wall even looked different without Lakshmi lying in it. No grunt of welcome nor faint light in eyes that had become rheumy with cataract. The blue-and-green striped blanket was neatly folded on top of the pillow. The floral bedsheet had been tautly straightened and tucked under the mattress, not a crease in sight.

Donna, Lakshmi's carer of three years, had made sure everything was in place. She stood in the corner, tears streaming down her smooth ebony skin. Laila took both Donna's hands in her own and squeezed hard. She willed herself not to cry. Not now. Not in front of her father and the neighbours who had crowded the dining room.

Her mother's two sisters were there too. Their presence had been scarce during Lakshmi's illness, as with the two other sisters living in New York. No phone call nor email in five years. They probably thought PSP was contagious, kept a wide berth. Lakshmi had been the eldest of five girls.

I come in peace, Laila wanted to say to her mother's siblings, but knew they wouldn't appreciate her humour. They were humourless at the best of times.

"Don't cry, Donna. You know that Mama wouldn't want that."

Donna struggled for words, but grief got the better of her. Gasping for breath, she left the room.

Laila wished she could leave the room like Donna, away from the encompassing grief and sorrow. Her aunts were staring in her direction. She could feel their eyes drilling holes in her back. Why should she go to comfort them? It should be the other way around. Lakshmi was her mother after all. Wasn't mother status higher than that of sister?

Deepa, the youngest aunt, glared in her direction. She was large-hipped and mean-faced. She had dedicated her life to religion. She drove the latest model car, lived in a beautiful house, wore the best clothes and flaunted the latest gadgets. She lived in the lap of luxury.

Laila often wondered what God thought of the likes of Deepa, who pretended to be pious but broke the first commandment every day by taking the Lord's name in vain to her own advantage. 'Do what I say and not what I do' applied perfectly to her. She attended daily mass but never had a kind word for anyone or an inkling of compassion. The good Lord wore sandals and rode a donkey. He didn't drive a Porsche Cayenne in fake Gucci ballerinas! It was the gospel according to Deepa. Laila disliked her more than Rani, the second-born, who'd admittedly never wiped Lakshmi's face nor changed her clothes but visited her every weekend.

Rani wasn't remotely queenly like her name suggested. Her parents had spent their meagre savings on educating her. She had several degrees and spoke five languages, and took every opportunity to point this out. She purposely started conversations in Italian, Spanish, German or French, knowing that the people she was addressing only spoke English or Hindi! She was fawning and feeble, never standing up for any family member financially nor emotionally. Her world revolved round Rohan, her son.

Kavita and Myla had moved to the United States many years ago. They had their own families, and had made a niche for themselves there. Money was what they lived and breathed. When they died, they would certainly be the richest people in the graveyard!

When Lakshmi had been well, they would visit often before going off on safari. The occasional Christmas card was stuffed with photographs of their apartments, personalised-license-plated cars and useless gadgets. Who wanted to see a photo of a sitting room with ostentatious furniture, a larger-than-life television, mobile phones, laptops or a swimming pool? Laila recalled Myla's scrawl on the back of one of the photos many years ago: "Yes, we have a swimming pool now."

"I'm sure she doesn't know how to swim," Laila had quipped. "Or is she too ugly to be in a photo?"

"No need to be nasty, Laila," Lakshmi had said sternly.

Laila had been proud of her jibe. She had secretly danced a jig in the dining room, away from Lakshmi's eyes.

Myla's children had been brought up in a material world. They were more interested in cars than their cousins. Not that it bothered Laila; she was happy to be left alone. She didn't want them keeping in touch with her for free rooms! Why flaunt her hotelier lifestyle? That would only make the green-eyed monster rear its head in her direction.

Low-key and discreet was how Laila liked her life. Didn't she have an Olympic-size swimming pool and one leisure pool in the hotel? Pity she couldn't be in both of them at the same time for a photo.

Kurt wasn't Catholic so when Laila had married him, there had been a huge uproar. "For heaven's sake," Laila had wanted to shout. "You don't have to be Catholic to be a good person. How many Catholics had committed atrocious acts? Bishops and cardinals included!" What went on in the Cardoso house was always their business. What went on in their houses was *solely* their business!

When Myla's son Mitesh lived out of wedlock, it was dropped into the conversation as a statement. Her fifteen-year-old daughter's pregnancy had been carefully hidden until innocent Devika confided in Lakshmi on one of their vacations to Kenya. The baby boy had been given up for adoption immediately after birth. Devika had no support from Myla, who refused to discuss the matter with her teenage daughter.

If anyone could relate to what her daughter had gone through, it should have been Myla, who had given up her own baby at the same age. A skeleton in the closet that Lakshmi had shared with Laila.

Lakshmi had only come to know of Kavita's son Nahar's divorce from a neighbour who knew a neighbour in New York. The rest of the family were under the impression that he was still happily married!

Kara, Tamer's wife, apparently didn't come from a good enough family, but no one pointed out that Arjun, Kavita's second son, changed partners on a regular basis and hadn't left the starting block on his elusive career.

Why couldn't her mother's side of the family be more like Amit's? They were back-benchers, unassuming, unambitious, minding their own business and getting on with their lacklustre lives.

There were no skeletons in their closets. Or were they so carefully guarded that no one knew of them?

Laila forcibly stopped herself from dwelling on the past. Neighbours took centre stage, coming to shake her hand or squeeze her shoulders. Everyone remembered Lakshmi's laughter. Her warm smile. Her friendly personality. Her simplicity. Her honesty. Her determination. Her generosity that knew no bounds. Her culinary skills. Her unshakeable faith in God, the church her sanctuary. Her kindness, most of all.

The ladies of the prayer group had lovely things to say. If only they'd had kind words when Lakshmi was alive and needed them.

Food was everywhere. *Sufurias* with chicken and beef curries, dhal and rice crowded the kitchen counter. There were loaves of bread and boxes of biscuits. Bunches of bananas, avocadoes, pineapples and papayas lay on the floor in yellow plastic carrier bags. At any other time, Laila would have feasted on the fruit. Why do people bring food at a time when the grieving have no appetite? There wasn't available space on the kitchen counters or on the round dining table. Still, the doorbell kept on ringing. More food accumulating.

The task of funeral arrangements landed on Laila's shoulders. Tamer would arrive tomorrow morning; lucky him! Resentment welled up like bile in Laila's throat.

"Have you gone to the printers? Don't forget to order the flowers! Is there enough food and drink?"

Being in England hadn't stopped Tamer from calling and texting. Just three weeks ago, she had received the same orders, for Lakshmi's birthday arrangements, then. Tamer had managed to arrive three days after the actual birth date. Exasperating!

Laila knew that had it been Tamer's in-laws, he would have been hands-on, full gallop ahead with all arrangements. Taking care of invitation cards, flowers, colour-coordinated tableware, and caterers. No detail would be left to chance. No excuses of shift work and no excuses of time off. Birthdays, anniversaries and other family occasions would be celebrated on the day, not a day or three later. Hell or high water, his mother- and father-in-law's birthday celebrations were a religious weekend away.

Today was not the day to count who had done what, when and where. Laila knew it would be a useless cause to fight over. Tamer always took the moral high road. He was always right.

At the funeral home, Laila stood staring at her mother's face. This was the woman she recognised. Peaceful. Serene. Beautiful. Calm. Gone was the woman who couldn't move. Whose facial expressions the illness had distorted. An illness that had robbed her of her beauty, her intelligence and her life. Now, Lakshmi looked like the goddess she had been named after. This was how Laila wanted to remember her.

Was that a smile on her lips, or was Laila imagining that Lakshmi was happy where she was? She touched her mother's face. It was cold, ice cold. Hard. Lifeless. So were her feet, and those once soft, tapered hands lay stiffly by her side. Laila placed her hands on her mother's chest. It was as hard as marble, and as cold, the lack of heartbeat unnerving. Laila drew back her hand. Her fingertips were icy cold, like her mother's lifeless body. It felt wrong that her mother was lying on a metal bed. Dead.

"Are you happy, Nan?" Laila whispered.

Since Lili and Lalita could speak, Laila had adopted "Nan" instead of "Mummy" when addressing Lakshmi. When PSP had deprived her mother of her voice, she had started using "my Mummy", as if the use of the possessive could perhaps jog Lakshmi's body into feeling how much Laila still needed her. Or had it been Laila's way of not accepting the illness? The use of that childlike phrase, "my Mummy", took her back to better times. Carefree days. Days of laughter. Days of joy. Happier days. How she would brag to her friends. My Mummy goes to work. My Mummy knows shorthand. My Mummy can dance. My Mummy has a beautiful voice; she sings in the church choir. My Mummy is the best cook. My Mummy can sew. My Mummy knitted this sweater for me.

The man at the funeral home had told Laila to take all the time she needed. He was one tap away behind the curtained window should she require anything.

Laila tapped at the window. The undertaker had a kindly face. He was tall and wiry with deep-set eyes. He looked at Laila like he genuinely felt her sorrow.

What a job, Laila thought. He dealt with death every day. Did he appreciate life more because of it?

"Could you please remove the hair on my mother's chin and upper lip? Can you make her look nice?"

Laila looked at her mother's unpainted toe- and fingernails. Lakshmi wouldn't want to leave this world looking like that. She had been particular about her looks, had been stylish all her life. She would never leave the house without pillar-box red or fuchsia-for-Lolita lipstick. Earrings and bangles were essential accessories for an Indian woman, the jingling an accompaniment as the day unfolded. The illness hadn't robbed her of trying to look good. She had insisted that her carer apply lipstick every morning after her shower.

"If I bring the nail polish, can you paint her nails and trim her eyebrows?" Laila asked.

"I have different coloured nail polish, madam. I'll use the red one. Don't worry. Your mother will look beautiful, like she is."

Laila swallowed the lump in her throat. The stranger's words had made her emotional. She felt weepy. She was tired.

"Do you have pink nail polish? Pink was my mother's favourite colour."

"Yes, madam, I have the colour. Also, I need the clothes you'll bury your mother in, and her shoes."

Laila nodded, not trusting herself to speak. Why the stiff upper lip in front of this man? He saw grief every day.

Before turning to leave, Laila fleetingly touched her mother's face. "Your time to rest, my Mummy."

Her eyes fell to the ring on her mother's finger. She fingered it lovingly. Lakshmi had worn it for fifty-four years.

"What's your name?" she asked the man.

"John Kamau."

"John, can you remove the wedding band on my mother's finger?"

With a tiny instrument, the ring was prised deftly from Lakshmi's stiff finger. John dropped it delicately into Laila's outstretched palm.

Lakshmi, love forever, Amit 3.6.50 was inscribed in the simple gold band. Laila slipped the ring next to her own wedding band. The colour contrast on her mother's finger where the ring had been was startling. An indelible mark. A sign of over fifty years of love. A permanent tattoo.

"What else is left to do, John?"

"You have to choose the coffin. Your father told me that your mother will be cremated. You'll need the urn. I'll show you the coffins, but we don't have urns. You can find them at Kim's Funeral Home."

John led the way down a corridor where coffins of different sizes and colours hung on rails. Some were richly lined, others plain. Dark wood, light wood, simple handles, ornate ones, in silver, gold and bronze. Laila stared, unable to make her choice. Someone had to do the job. She couldn't have asked her father, who seemed so fragile, replaced by a shrivelled old man who sat at Lakshmi's place on the sofa, his head in his hands.

John Kamau was rambling off prices. Laila pointed to a coffin. Dark red in colour, cotton-lined, reasonably priced. There wasn't any point spending money that would go up in flames. Ever the realist.

Next the hearse. There was a choice of a black or white one. Laila settled on the white.

"Tomorrow, your family has to be here early enough. You say your last goodbyes before we drive the body to the church." John quietly explained the procedure. "After the mass, the body will be taken to the crematorium. On Monday, you can collect the urn with the ashes."

The body. That was what he called her mother. It sounded like a title of a horror movie.

Laila could feel the beginning of a headache. When would it stop? Her mother lay two rooms away, lifeless, while she made funeral plans. If only the clock could go back to happier times or move forward rapidly so that this would be behind her. A magic wand would have come in handy. Wave everything away.

"Sign here, here and here," John said, pointing to the dotted line.

Laila blindly signed at the bottom of each page. She realised on the last page that she had used her maiden name, Cardoso.

***

Resting her head on the steering wheel of the old dusty blue Toyota, Laila wished she could stay there. Was it possible to get over the death of a loved one? Does life ever go back to normality? Would the heavy weight on her heart lessen with time? Too many questions, too few answers. Shaking herself out of her reverie, Laila started the car. The clock on the dashboard read 2:33 p.m. She had arrived that morning at 5:00 a.m. Unbelievable how much could get done in a matter of hours, unpleasant as the chore was. She still had to get the urn, pass by the church to speak to the priest, rush to the printers for the booklets with the readings and hymns.

Flowers! Laila had forgotten the wreath. No flowers had been requested in the newspaper obituary, donations instead to PSP research. Lakshmi had asked for white carnations. Carnations, so associated with death, Laila thought morbidly. She settled on white and yellow daisies. Happy flowers. Sorry, my Mummy. I know I'm not abiding to your request.

Laila didn't like carnations, but Lakshmi did. That's what Lakshmi had wanted. It would be the last thing Laila would ever do for her mother. Why not grant her last request?

"Can you finish off the wreath with white carnations?"

The florist looked at Laila impatiently. It was past closing time.

Laila had put her foot in the shop in the nick of time. "What?" Laila wanted to shout at her. "My mother is dead. Dead. Can you understand that?"

She had to get a grip. It wasn't the florist's fault. It was after 6:00 p.m. on a Friday. The world hadn't come to an end because Laila had lost her mother. Lakshmi Cardoso was no more, but the world continued to turn.

Laila returned to the house a little after seven. The sitting room was heaving with people, as was the dining room. There were a few familiar faces. Amit looked helplessly at Laila, the relief obvious on his face. It was kind of people to want to remember Lakshmi and to grieve with them, but in most cases the grieving just wanted to be left alone. Alone with the memories. The regrets. The pain. To wail and rant at the unfairness of life. Wouldn't it be better to congregate a few months later? Thinking about the departed would be easier. Less painful. Happy memories, sharper.

Laila thought of the Khalil Gibran quote, "Some of you say joy is greater than sorrow, and others say, nay, sorrow is the greater. But I say unto you, they are inseparable. Together they come, and when one sits alone with you at your board, remember that the other is asleep upon your bed."

Tamer arrived just after 10:00 p.m., his wife Kara and ten-year-old twin sons Matthew and Michael in tow. Where had the closeness she and Tamer had shared disappeared to?

When she had started her periods, it was Tamer she had run to. She had been too shy to talk to Lakshmi. Tamer, who had explained to her the changes in her body. Tamer, who had rushed out to buy the packet of Stayfree pads. Tamer, who finally told Lakshmi.

Growing up, they had been each other's shadows. Six years separated them. She and Tamer had been so in tune with each other. Laila had pretended they were twins in school. Each one an extension of the other.

Their childhood bond had evaporated with his marriage.

Yes, marriage changed people. Men, it seemed, embraced their wife's families completely. Was it fear of confrontation? Could the change be so drastic as to make her brother unrecognisable? Did Tamer think the same about her?

Laila hugged him briefly.

"How was the flight?" She felt the need to make small talk as the silence stretched. If only Kara would leave the room.

Kara was a successful career woman; however, on the home front she was incapable of making decisions herself. Tamer's stamp of validation was on every minute household detail. Kara knew her helplessness burgeoned Tamer's ego.

Laila would have liked to have a few moments alone with her brother to remember their mother. It was not to be. She knew Tamer was hurting—Lakshmi had meant the world to him—but she couldn't interact with her brother with Kara as a spectator.

**

Laila stared at the bedroom ceiling. Sleep had eluded her the whole night. There were too many memories in this room she'd grown up in. The bedcover and curtains she had chosen with Lakshmi on her sixteenth birthday, with their different shades of pink palm branches. She had been deliriously happy with the room makeover. The white paint was flaking now in the corner. The room looked tired.

The beige net curtains hang limply, several hooks missing. The house was crumbling, sorely lacking Lakshmi's touch. No amount of house help would restore it to its former glory.

Laila could hear her father splashing water over his face in the bathroom opposite. It was 6:00 a.m.

It was going to be a long day.

At the funeral home, Tamer collapsed on seeing Lakshmi. The aunties were near at hand to prop him up.

"Don't cry, Tamer," Rani repeated over and over.

"I'm so sorry for your loss, Tamer. You were your mother's favourite," Deepa said, trying to console her nephew.

What about my tears? What about my loss? Laila thought angrily. When did Tamer become Lakshmi's favourite? Laila took a deep breath.

She hadn't even got a nod in her direction yesterday. Today, they stubbornly blanked her out. Rani and Deepa disliked her. The feeling was reciprocated.

Laila ignored the commotion and walked over to where her mother lay in the coffin she had chosen. John Kamau had done a great job. Lakshmi looked like an angel. Her face was calm and restful. Asleep. Laila slowly walked around the coffin, touching her mother gently, starting from her feet. Lakshmi wore her favourite clothes. A pink sweater, brown slacks and her brown and gold sandals. She had loved this outfit. A string of pink beads and pink bangles on her wrists. Tiny pink studs in her ears. Her finger and toenails were painted a beautiful baby pink, and John had even applied pink lipstick. Laila made a mental note to come back to thank him.

Amit stood at the head of the coffin. The sorrow on his face was tangible. No tears. Just raw pain.

Weirdly, Laila wondered if she would bury Kurt or would it be the other way around. How do you say goodbye to someone you've cherished and cared for? Watched over through sickness and health for over fifty years?

Kara was trying in vain to comfort Tamer, who was inconsolable. Laila wanted to shake him. Their father had lost his wife, and he was dignified.

The church was packed; Mama Mboga Esther, the vegetable lady, was there, without her heavy baskets of vegetables and fruits. She plied the hot, dusty streets of the suburbs of Nairobi selling her groceries. She knew what each customer needed from okra to drumsticks to white gourd, fresh bunches of coriander, mint and parsley. Lakshmi had been a good client. During her illness, Esther would pass by daily just to wave to her from the gate as Lakshmi sat rigidly in the sun. Amit had started buying vegetables and fruit from the supermarket, but that hadn't stopped Esther's daily visits.

Esther walked up to the coffin and placed a bunch of *dhania* on it. The baksheesh of coriander she always gave Lakshmi.

"Go well, Mama Lakshmi," she whispered.

The mass was beautiful, as was the singing. After Tamer's poignant eulogy, Rohan walked up to the pulpit. He whipped out of his coat pocket a box of readymade crème caramel. Laila knew whatever came out of his mouth would irritate her. It always did.

"Aunty Lakshmi will always be remembered for this. Her favourite dessert."

Laila gripped the pew until her knuckles turned white. He rambled on about Lakshmi and her life, like he knew every detail. Laila thought she would explode. Why did her cousin Rohan crave the limelight? This wasn't 'Kenya's Got Talent'.

It wasn't the first time he had usurped a family gathering. He loved making speeches. His effeminate traits were more pronounced as he stood there with the Birds Delight box. Lakshmi loved homemade crème caramel with fresh eggs and milk, not this awful, powdery shop-bought concoction that had no taste.

Where had they been when Lakshmi couldn't turn or walk? Rohan and his mother, Rani, would come to pat Lakshmi on the head. She wasn't a dog. The visit would last five minutes. They were too afraid that they would have to feed or bathe her, God forbid change her pamper.

Had he forgotten his nasty email of a few months ago? There'd been no love for Lakshmi in that.

Laila knew she wasn't liked. She was too frank. Too honest for their liking. She never hid her animosity toward her mother's side of the family.

Lakshmi had been protective of her siblings. She loved them, faults and all. She knew they didn't treat her fairly, but it didn't matter. She loved them unconditionally. Laila remembered the numerous battles she'd had with her mother in the days before her illness.

"Why do you stand up for them when they treat you so appallingly? They keep secrets from you. Do you know when and where they go on vacation? Do they think we'll ask to join them? They leave you out of so much. They have fancy dinners and lunches, but do they invite you? Are they ashamed of you? I don't even know why you bother to talk to them." Laila had rambled.

"They're my sisters, Laila my child. Don't talk about them like that. Family is important. As the eldest, I have to stand by them."

"Ma, can you hear yourself? *They* have the right to talk to you any way they want. *They* come round uninvited, conveniently at lunchtime, but never invite us in return. *They* place orders for what you should cook for them without providing a single ingredient. *They* go back and forth to India, only informing you when they're about to step on the plane. When we were going through hard times, did they spare a shilling to help us? How often do their children call *you*? Tamer and I have to write to them once a month. We are yet to get a reply."

The constant arguments Laila remembered having with Lakshmi in her teen years were always about her aunties.

"Secrets and lies. That's where your sisters' talents lie," Laila had shouted one Saturday afternoon.

Deepa, Rani, Kavita and Myla had been thorns in Laila's side for far too long. Their children hadn't called Lakshmi once during her illness, not even a note nor a card.

Laila couldn't decide who of the three, Rani, Rohan or Deepa, she disliked the most.

Laila had asked Rohan on one of her visits why his mum couldn't do more for her sister. Why she dropped in on Amit, who wasn't the patient, every day at the office.

"At least Mum is in the same country," Rohan retorted, nostrils flaring. "You drop in to visit your mum every few months and only for a few days at a time."

A few weeks later, Laila had received an email that was copied to Tamer and Kara.

Subj: Peace to you

That is my wish to you all for this year and always.

Because for sure it seems that there isn't much around at the moment.

Guys, we're none of us perfect. Not me. Not my mum. And not any of you. Let's remember that. So my mum is hard-headed and likes to prove her point when she feels she's right! But she's not the mad one, is she? As in, 'institutionalised' mad.

As for staying away from your dad in the office. I guess Mum will just be joining the lot of you then, in the staying-away part, I mean.

It's a shame that "family" can deteriorate this way but hey, God is always in control and knows what is best for us all. It would be great if all "shit" can stay where it belongs—in the toilet—but if it doesn't, I'm sure the sewers can spew their contents both directions.

Have a blessed year.

Rohan

Laila couldn't believe the anger she was capable of. It was by sheer effort that she hadn't replied to the email. Tamer had ignored it—no confrontation for him. He was the golden boy in the family's eyes, winning all the popularity contests, not like devil-woman Laila!

Lakshmi had suffered a nervous breakdown years ago; that was what Rohan had alluded to. She had been out of a job for two years. Funds were low, and they could barely make ends meet. Strong Lakshmi had succumbed to the pressure.

Rohan belonged in the sewer he'd talked about. Predictably, God had been brought into the equation.

This was the same boy Lakshmi had loved with all her heart. He was an Aquarian; it was his way or no way!

Not once during those difficult years had money been forthcoming from either Rani or Deepa. Myla and Kavita played out of sight, out of mind. Why should they worry about their struggling sister? Their cups were overflowing in the land of opportunity.

"Why don't you take one last family photo?" Rohan stood with the camera poised on a limp arm. The mass had just ended.

His ramblings had mercifully come to an end after fifteen long minutes. Laila's hand itched to slap his face. There were fifteen years between them, but Rohan behaved like he was fifty years older. He charmed his way out of tight situations as easily as an oily cobra, the coy grin meant to make up for the cruel, insensitive words.

Laila looked at Tamer. Had she heard right? A last family photo with a coffin. How many of those do you see on mantelpieces or coffee tables?

Tamer was in a world of his own. Kara, as usual, looked to him for approval. Amit duly stood by the coffin. Tamer followed in a daze with Kara, Michael and Matthew in tow.

As it's a last family photo, I might as well smile, Laila thought.

Friends filed past, whispering condolences and remembrances of Lakshmi's life.

People hadn't understood the disease. Furtive glances had accompanied Lakshmi when she entered public places. No eye contact. Many thought she belonged in a mental asylum. When a disease is not understood, it's convenient to label it as insanity, the easiest explanation.

Lakshmi had always been the life of every party, outing or gathering. She had loved singing and dancing. She had loved life. Why had life robbed her of five years?

The crematorium was a private gathering with family only. There was no priest to officiate. It wasn't Catholic to cremate. If only Laila could wave a magic wand to make Rani, Rohan and Deepa disappear. She didn't want them anywhere near her mother. They were never close to her in life; why pretend in death?

Laila stood looking down at her mother's peaceful face. There was the smile again. *Go well, my Mummy. I'll miss you.*

Tamer had chosen "Wind Beneath My Wings" by Bette Midler as the last song. As the words of the song filled the enclosed space, Laila wished she had told her mother that she had been her hero. Her heroine.

Laila jumped as the lid of the coffin was closed. Finality. The End.

Kara was consoling Tamer, who had broken down once again.

Amit was inconsolable. He held a handkerchief, startlingly white against his brown skin, against his eyes as he tried to contain the sobs wracking his body. The sobs gradually subsided while Laila stood awkwardly patting her father's shoulder. She wanted to hug him but didn't know how.

Lakshmi had told her often to love more, not to hide behind a glass window, but Laila couldn't. It was her protection. A barrier from getting hurt. It was safer this way.

"Let's go home, Daddy," Laila whispered, swallowing the lump in her throat.

Today, again, she had kept a tight rein over her emotions. She would mourn her mother alone.

Soft tears rolled down Amit's cheeks. He didn't brush them away but turned to look out of the window. Laila knew the road ahead would be long and winding without Lakshmi at the helm.

CHAPTER 2

"THERE MUST BE MORE TO LIFE THAN THIS"

December 1970

Laila sat on the bottom cement step outside the front door. The grass needed to be cut. On any other day she would have got to work with the cutlass. Chopping at the long blades, throwing in all her energy, loving the rich, mossy smell of freshly cut grass. Cutting grass had started out as a chore. Something to occupy her vacation days.

"You can't be idle the whole day, Laila," Lakshmi had told her. "Try cutting the grass. It will keep you busy and reduce your father's weekend tasks."

"But Mummy, why can't Tamer do it?"

"Because I am asking you. Tamer has to study for his exams at the end of the year."

Today she was in no mood to see the cut strands of grass flying over her shoulders, sticking to her curly hair or her clothes.

Blackie, her spaniel, licked the tears from her cheeks. Laila imagined that he was confused why his mistress hadn't spent time playing and kissing him today. She had come home from school and ignored him. He gave a short bark to get her attention.

Laila stroked Blackie's ear absently. All she wanted was for Lakshmi to come home from work. After what seemed like forever, she finally saw her mother push open the heavy, black iron gate.

She looked exhausted. Her navy blue shoes were red with dust from walking the marram roads. The frayed strap of her black handbag hung limply from her shoulder, the *Daily Nation* rolled up in her hand. Laila debated whether to tell her mother now or later, after she had her tea. She decided later would be best.

"How come you're out in the hot sun, Laila?" Lakshmi patted Laila's cheek. "Don't you have any homework today? Have you been crying, my child?" She held Laila's small chin, staring into her daughter's eyes.

"I'm fine, Ma." Laila forced a smile. Her mouth was dry; she could hardly swallow her saliva. She knew her mother longed for the much-needed cup of tea after her day at work. It wouldn't be right to tell her now.

"You sure, my child?"

Laila nodded. She needed to tell her mother before her father came home from work. She still had an hour. How would she start? She was confused herself. She felt so dirty. After her shower, she had felt a little better, but the shower had been cold. Lakshmi only allowed the hot water to be turned on on Saturdays and Wednesdays, to save on electricity.

Today, Mr Fernando, the next door neighbour, had been outside the school gates. Zoe, his daughter, was in the same class as Laila and hadn't been well the last two days. Laila wondered why he was there but walked off, ignoring him.

School was only a five-minute walk from home.

"Laila, I have a message for you from Zoe," he said as he rolled down the car window. "It's important." He smiled encouragingly at her.

Laila walked to the white sedan.

She had known Mr Fernando all her life. Zoe was her best friend. She had four older brothers who were already married, and their age difference was so great that they had nothing in common with her. It was Laila who she walked to school with, played dolls with and studied with.

"Zoe is in hospital. She's asking for you. I'll take you to see her." He smiled, showing uneven teeth. "Come, we won't be long."

Laila knew that she shouldn't go without asking Lakshmi first, but surely her mother wouldn't mind. Lakshmi knew how close she was with Zoe.

Why was Zoe in hospital? She had a cold a few days ago, nothing serious.

Laila's young brain weighed the outcome of getting into the car. A few minutes to cheer Zoe up couldn't be so bad. She grabbed the door handle.

"See you tomorrow, Laila," Janet, the girl who sat next to her in class, shouted, waving madly.

Laila waved back, sticking her tongue out and crossing her eyes. She was known to be the most innovative grimace-maker in the entire school.

"What's wrong with Zoe, Uncle? I thought she had a cold. Why is she in hospital?"

"You'll see. First, let's stop by the shops to buy some chocolates for the two of you."

The shops were down the road. Laila wasn't fond of chocolates, preferring the powdery glucose sweets. She didn't dare tell her friends; they would think her strange. Who didn't like chocolates? Perhaps if she ate them more often the taste would grow on her, but that was out of the question. There was no place for chocolates on Lakshmi's tight budget.

Unlike most of her friends, Laila's parents struggled to make ends meet. Just last week, Laila had squirmed when she had been called to Sister Ruth's office. Her school fees had been long overdue. Lakshmi had pled with the Irish headmistress not to send Laila home. She promised that she would settle the outstanding amount at the end of the month.

"Mrs Cardoso, if I allow you an extension, then I will have to make exceptions for other parents. Please understand," Sister Ruth reasoned.

Lakshmi dropped to her knees. She clutched Sister Ruth's stockinged ankles. "I'm begging you, Sister Ruth. Please let my Laila stay in class, only for the next two weeks. I promise that at the end of the month you'll have the school fees."

Laila had wanted the floor to open and swallow her whole. How could her mother beg? What was she doing? Thankfully there had been no one around except for the secretary, Muthoni, a rotund African lady with a huge afro, which was tamed with a yellow satin ribbon.

Sister Ruth's fair, freckled complexion turned beetroot. Her arms that had a few moments ago been tightly folded below her chest, were now limp by her side.

"Mrs Cardoso, please stand."

Lakshmi didn't budge. She knelt, her head bowed.

"Please. I'm begging you, Sister Ruth."

"Alright, Mrs Cardoso. Laila can stay in school. Two more weeks. No more. Do you understand?" The colour slowly receded from Sister Ruth's freckled cheeks. "Please don't tell any other parent what I've done for you." Ruth stared sternly at Lakshmi and held out her hand for Lakshmi to pull herself up.

"Thank you. I'll never forget your kindness. God bless you, Sister Ruth."

Lakshmi stood. She tried to hold Laila's hand as they left the office, but Laila was having none of it. How could her mother have embarrassed her? How could she not afford 150 shillings? Many of her classmates were getting 100 shillings as pocket money. Laila strode off. She didn't want any of her friends to see her with her mother. Suddenly Lakshmi's worn-out sweater and ugly, dusty flat shoes had been too much to bear.

Other mothers came to school in high heels. Beautifully made up, smelling of perfume. Lakshmi only wore lipstick and often smelled of sweat. She walked everywhere to save on bus fare. If Laila was honest, she knew that Lakshmi could outshine any of the mothers when she had her hair blow-dried, her nails painted and her Sunday clothes on, a bright red scarf around her neck or in her hair. Unlike other mothers, Lakshmi didn't need layers of foundation to mask patchy, wrinkly skin.

Lakshmi was the only Indian mother who worked. The others stayed at home to cook and supervise the housemaid. They went shopping together and drank tea at quaint cafes in town. They had manicures, pedicures and long massages to while away the hours. Their husbands were managers in insurance companies or banks or ran their own automobile or retail business.

"Why was your mother at Sister Ruth's office?" Janet asked Laila during the afternoon break.

"I don't know. Why are you so nosy?" Laila snapped.

Janet was tall and lanky for an eleven-year-old. She was light-skinned for a Kikuyu, almost the same colour as Laila. Her neatly braided hair held a fascination for Laila. Every Monday the neat rows would be braided into a different style, sometimes with black thread or colourful beads. Laila dreamed of having Janet's hairdresser work on her curly hair, from frizz to fabulous.

"Stay cool. I was only asking. Keep your bad mood to yourself, Laila Cardoso," Janet retorted, walking away in a huff.

Laila leaned against the wall. She knew that she shouldn't have bitten Janet's head off. It wasn't Janet's fault her mother couldn't afford school fees.

It was so unfair. How come Tamer's fees were always paid on time? Tears rolled down Laila's fair cheeks. She wished she could run away.

Why couldn't her parents be rich like Zoe's? They never seemed to lack for anything. Zoe had birthday parties, new dresses every month, and even leather shoes, unlike the plastic ones Laila wore, her feet clammy with sweat. Zoe could barely close her lunchbox. It was full with chocolates and sweets, crisps, popcorn and real orange juice. She ate ham and cheese sandwiches while Laila had to make do with jam sandwiches, a banana and horrible orange squash.

Life was *so* unfair.

Mr Fernando got into the car with a bulging brown paper bag. He tossed it onto Laila's lap. "For you."

Laila's eyes were saucers. The bag was full with Dairy Milk chocolates. Milk and dark, fruit and nut, hazelnut and walnut. Mars bars, Kit-Kats, lollipops, bubble gum, gummy bears, jelly beans. The treats in the bag would last her a long time, even if she shared them with Tamer. He would be delirious with joy; he loved anything sweet.

Laila lifted her head out of the bag. They weren't driving on the main road.

"This is not the way to the hospital, Uncle. Where are we going?"

Mr Fernando was driving on the Marram Road leading toward the nearby national park. He didn't bother answering Laila.

The park was close to school. Students and teachers took for granted the wildlife they saw on a daily basis from the classroom's bay windows. Zebra, giraffe and numerous herds of antelope, from kudus to eland and Thompson gazelles, grazed in the open field at the back of the school. Baboons and even elephants were a common sight. If they were lucky they would spot lions, and once they saw a leopard crouching in the long grass, ready for a kill. The mesmerised silence in the classroom had turned to loud shouts and banging on the glass windows. The noise emanating from the all-girls classroom had been enough to galvanise the impala to flee in large leaps and bounds. The leopard slouched back to the national park, frustrated at having his lunch snatched from him.

"Where are we going, Uncle?" Laila asked again. She was nervous.

Something wasn't right. Why had Mr Fernando brought her down this lonely road? There was nobody around. The grass was long on either side of the road. The main road was in the distance. Laila could just make out the cars zooming past.

The silence stretched. He continued to drive.

Finally, the car stopped.

Mr Fernando pressed a button, and the click of the doors locking alarmed Laila. It was a modern car, unlike Amit's, that had to be locked manually with a key. What was going on? Every pore in her body oozed sweat. Her hands were cold. Her upper lip had tiny beads of perspiration. Laila clutched the door handle. Mr Fernando's face loomed closer.

Laila turned to look out of the car window. There was no one around.

"Don't be afraid, Laila. Your uncle isn't going to hurt you." His jaundiced eyes looked lasciviously at her.

Laila could see the long grey hairs sticking out from his bulbous nose, red veins clearly visible. His lips were dry and flaking. His eyes the colour of dirty dishwater, the lashes sparse.

Slowly he stroked Laila's arm. His fingernails were long. Laila winced. He smiled and licked his lips. Laila thought she would faint. She tried to pull her arm away, but Mr Fernando held her tight. Suddenly, he grabbed Laila's delicate neck and shoved his tongue into her mouth. He smelt of onions and curry. Laila gagged. This only made uncle's tongue probe deeper into her mouth. His hands grabbed at Laila's budding breasts. He squeezed hard at the nipples. Tears streamed down Laila's cheeks.

"Stop moving, you stupid girl." Mr Fernando spoke through gritted teeth. His tongue was no longer in her mouth.

"Please stop. Uncle, stop, please." Laila realised she was begging. The way Lakshmi had. He ignored her.

Her respite was short-lived. Again, in and out his tongue went, biting her bottom lip. Squeezing at her breasts. Uncle was strong. A short, stout man with a flabby paunch. Laila's lime-green uniform dress rose up her legs. She felt Mr Fernando's hand touch her panties. What was he doing? Tears were coming fast now. Sobs.

He grabbed Laila's hand and placed it on the front of his trousers as he reached for the zip. Laila thought she would pass out. Her head was reeling. Was she being held underwater? It felt like hot bubbles were bursting in her brain, running out through her ears, eyes and nose.

A noise was coming from a distance. Louder. An urgent rapping on the window. Uncle pushed Laila away. Laila turned her tear-streaked face toward the window. A wizened old man stood there. His cane held against the glass.

"*Fungua dirisha.*" Open the window. He spoke softly but firmly.

There were beads of sweat on Mr Fernando's Brylcreemed receding hairline. The dark patch of perspiration was obvious under the armpits of his white shirt. The old man rapped on the window again. Waving his cane angrily.

"Bloody Africans. Can't mind their own business," Mr Fernando spat out. His face was black with rage. "Stupid people." He fumbled with the ignition. The car started on the second try. He reversed furiously down the road, just missing the mzee by a few centimetres. "Don't you dare breathe a word of this to anyone. No one will believe you anyway. They'll call you a little liar." He was breathless as he spat out the sentences. Onion breath wafted in the confines of the car.

His trousers hung around his large waist. The belt was unfastened and the top button gaped open. His creased shirt had rolled up in the struggle and

Laila could make out his brown flesh. The white vest underneath was murky brown with dirt and sweat. His underwear had a dark wet stain.

Laila shuddered uncontrollably.

They had reached school. No one was around. The grey gate was closed.

"Get out, you bitch. Remember, one word from me and your father will lose his job." His eyeballs bulged from their sockets. The brown irises furious.

It wasn't an empty threat. Mr Fernando worked at the same offices as Amit, only higher up.

Laila stumbled out of the car. She threw up. Revulsion clung to her tiny body, making her shudder, the smell of onions strong in her mouth.

The thud of the brown paper bag made her jump. It landed neatly at her feet.

"Not one word out of you," Mr Fernando yelled, driving off with screeching brakes.

Laila stood under the shade of the pepper trees that lined the school entrance. Fat green caterpillars covered most of the branches. She breathed in deeply. She wanted desperately to brush her teeth. Why had Uncle done that to her? She felt dirty. She felt sick. A hundred hammers were banging in her head, each hitting harder than the last. Her head would explode. Would the pain ever recede? She would tell Lakshmi. Lakshmi always knew what to do.

Laila had picked up the brown paper bag and weaved her way home like a drunkard. Confused. Dazed. Sick. Angry. Sad.

"Laila, what are you telling me?" The horror on Lakshmi's face was obvious. "Are you sure, my child?" She stroked Laila's cheek and her long black hair.

Laila had never seen her mother this upset. The frown between her brows was deep. Tears brimmed in her caramel eyes. Lakshmi never cried.

"Oh my Jesus, help us," she kept repeating.

Laila brought out the bag of sweets and chocolates from under her bed. "He gave me this."

Tears spilled from Lakshmi's eyes, pain written in them.

Drawing Laila close to her, Lakshmi hugged her daughter. She held her for a long time without saying a word.

Today, Lakshmi's sweat was comforting. Laila felt the anger and hate toward Mr Fernando lessen. She could hear the thump-thump of Lakshmi's rapidly beating heart. Hot teardrops landed on her hair.

"Laila, what Mr Fernando did to you was wrong. Very wrong. Do you understand?"

Laila nodded. Mother and daughter sat in silence again, Lakshmi stroking Laila's long dark hair.

Long minutes passed before Lakshmi spoke again. "My child, we can't say anything to anyone about this. Especially not your father. He'll kill him. Promise me that you'll never breathe a word of this. Please." She looked pleadingly at Laila.

"But why, Mummy? I want Daddy to kill him."

"Because, Laila! It will cause problems. Many problems that we can do without. Mostly your father needs his job. Do you understand?"

Laila nodded. She didn't understand. She wanted to scream. She knew this was wrong. How could that horrible fat uncle do this to her?

"I hate him, Mummy." Laila wanted to kick the wall. She needed to vent her anger and frustration on someone, on something. Anything.

Instead, she nodded again. Laila would promise anything just to stop her mother's tears. Lakshmi was stronger than an oak. Nothing or no one could faze her. If Lakshmi was crying, it had to be serious, very serious.

Even when she'd begged Sister Ruth, she hadn't cried.

Laila wiped her mother's tears with the palms of her small hands. "Stop crying, Mummy. I won't tell. I won't tell anyone. Not Daddy and not even Tamer."

Lakshmi hugged her daughter tight. Her tears were subsiding.

"One more thing, Laila. From now on you're not allowed to go anywhere near Mr Fernando's house."

"But Mummy, how will I play with Zoe?"

"Zoe can come here. You can play in school."

"But Zoe's garden is bigger, and there are trees there that we can climb and bushes we can hide behind."

"Laila, listen to me, my child. You're no longer allowed to go there. Do you want Mr Fernando to do what he did today again?"

Laila shuddered. She shook her head vehemently.

"Good girl. Then *don't* ever go there. Do you understand?"

Laila nodded forlornly. She loved playing in Zoe's garden. Especially climbing the Jacaranda tree, both of them perched in the branches like lazy lionesses.

"'I'm so sorry, my child. What happened today was wrong and should never have happened. I'm sorry I couldn't have protected you."

"Why are you sorry, Mummy? You didn't do anything."

Lakshmi smiled sadly at Laila. "It's because I didn't do anything. One day you'll understand why

I'm sorry. I love you very much, Laila. Remember that always."

The sound of Amit's car made Lakshmi stand up hastily. She wiped her eyes on her sweater. "Remember, Laila, this is our secret." She put a finger to her full lips.

Laila sat staring at the chocolates. The brown paper bag was creased. There was a tiny tear at the bottom. The urge to throw them into the bin was strong, but that would be stupid. Such expensive goodies. No, she would give them to Tamer. He could eat them all or share some with his friends tomorrow at break time.

She grabbed the bag and took it to his room.

"Whoa! Where did you get these?" Tamer's eyes sparkled in delight, and Laila shrugged. "Don't you want to keep any?"

"No. You can have them all." She didn't want to keep sweets that she had paid a price for.

***

In the weeks that followed, Laila's bubbly nature was replaced by a reserved, dull quiet child.

Father Kelly, the Irish priest, remarked on her silence one Saturday afternoon after the catechism class. "How come you're so quiet lately, Laila? What's happened to the chatterbox I know?" His deep blue eyes had twinkled kindly.

Father Kelly was tall but rotund, making him look stocky. He had a balding pate, similar to the monks of yore. He could easily pass for Friar John in *Robin Hood*. He was whiter than white, with the two red patches on his cheeks a sign of never acclimatising to the Kenyan heat even after twenty-five years of calling the country home. He often said he missed the rain and cold of his small Irish village, but spent every afternoon on the veranda of his parish house basking in the African sunshine or rain with a stack of books, a cup of tea and two cookies.

Laila's constant chatting or laughing during his sermons was missed, even though once he had stormed out of the confessional box because Laila had a fit of laughter for no reason.

"Laila, leave my church immediately," he had boomed angrily, pointing at the imposing wooden doors. "Once you've controlled yourself, only then you'll be welcomed back."

Laila had slipped out of the church chortling.

"Do you want to tell me something?" he asked now. "Is everything okay at home? You're not yourself lately, my child." He sounded like Lakshmi. He laid a plump hand on Laila's head.

"Everything is fine, Father." Laila put on her brightest smile. She couldn't confide in him. She had promised Lakshmi.

She needed time to forget. She would be okay in time.

***

September 2012

Where had the years gone? Laila thought as she removed her tortoise-shell glasses and rubbed the bridge of her nose. The familiar ringtone on her iPhone told her that Tamer was calling.

"You okay, Laila?" Tamer didn't wait for a reply. "Do you remember Mr Fernando?" he asked.

How could she forget?

"What about him?" Laila asked dully. Why would she be interested?

"I just got a call from Zoe. He passed away last night. He was ninety-eight. Can you imagine? The family is heartbroken."

Laila had stopped listening to Tamer ramble on. The 'uncle' she had trusted was dead. No big loss; he was a dirty old man.

What he had done to her had bothered her through her teenage years. She had pushed the incident to the back of her mind, not letting it mark her life. Many evenings when she and Tamer would be sitting on the sofa listening to their favourite radio show, Sundowner with Jeffery Kinuthia, she would open her mouth to confide in her brother but then think better of it. She had made a promise to Lakshmi not to tell.

Tamer had been good friends with Zoe's brothers. She wouldn't be able to bear it if he chose to continue his friendship with them knowing what Mr Fernando had done to her. It had been easier this way. He didn't have to make a choice that could hurt her.

It hurt nonetheless.

What had happened forty years ago came rushing back like yesterday. Laila shuddered. The death of a family member was a loss all-encompassing, but she couldn't bring herself to feel sorry for Zoe or her family, even after all the years.

"Laila, you're not listening. Will you send Zoe an email?" Tamer waited for an answer. "Laila?"

"Why?"

"What do you mean, why? Didn't you hear what I said?"

"I heard you, Tamer. Yes, I will. Maybe."

"What do you mean, maybe? They were our neighbours for years."

"I know that!"

The conversation was pointless. She knew Tamer would nag her till she agreed to do what he wanted.

"Laila, what happened between you and Zoe when we were growing up?" he asked. "Why did you suddenly go off her? What was the sin she committed for you to stop talking to her?"

Not *her* sin, but Laila didn't want to explain. Not after all this time. There was no point in digging into the past. Let sleeping dogs lie.

"I'll send the email, Tamer," Laila lied, ending the conversation.

She thought of Zoe, who had pestered her for years on why she wouldn't come over to play.

"Laila, your garden is so small. You don't have even one tree for us to climb."

"Both our books can't fit on this tiny desk."

"I have a coloured television. Why are we watching Scooby Doo on your black and white TV?"

Laila had run out of excuses. She knew it wasn't Zoe's fault, but she'd begun to resent her best friend.

Their friendship could never be the same.

They drifted apart, until they stopped talking completely. Every girl in school whispered about their friendship.

"How come you don't talk to Zoe?" Janet had demanded again. "How come you don't walk home together? Why do you sit far from Zoe at break time? Why have you stopped playing with Zoe?"

Janet was persistent.

Laila remained a wall.

Finally, Janet gave up asking.

Many times, Laila spotted Mr Fernando lurking in his garden or in the vicinity of the school. Whenever she did, she ran as fast as her legs could carry her. Once, he followed her from school in his car at snail speed, trying to entice her to get into the vehicle. The brown paper bag stuffed with sweets and chocolates, the lure.

Lakshmi had never mentioned the incident. Nor had Laila. But her mother was never the same with the Fernandos, Laila noticed. She spoke only when absolutely necessary to Mrs Fernando and practically never to Mr Fernando.

Laila missed Zoe sorely, but even at such a young age she'd known that life went on; there wasn't any point of dwelling on negative things. She was thankful to the wizened old man. If he hadn't appeared at the car window like a guardian angel, her fate would have been worse.

"You needn't have blamed yourself for doing nothing," Laila whispered. "You needn't have felt sorry. I'm okay, Mummy."

CHAPTER 3

"JUST LIKE A PILL"

March 1973

"She's manipulative. Can't you see that, my child?" Lakshmi tried reasoning with fourteen-year-old Laila.

Laila stared defiantly at her mother. Her blood boiling. She had to keep her teenage self in check or she would explode.

Why did Lakshmi pick on Urvashi? Why didn't she like her? It irked Laila that her mother couldn't see eye to eye with her new best friend. Urvashi had arrived at school a couple of months ago. Her family had moved from Cape Town to Kenya to expand her father's growing uniform business.

"You always have something nasty to say about her. Why do you want me to stop seeing her? You're jealous. I know you are." Laila was like most teenagers—petulant and argumentative in equal measures. She had an answer for everything, fourteen going on forty.

"Why would I be jealous, Laila? And don't raise your voice at me. One day you'll regret this friendship. Mark my words."

Laila made faces behind her mother's back. *I'll mark nothing*, she thought stubbornly. She would give Lakshmi a few days to calm down. She always did in the end.

Laila would have to tell Urvashi not to come round for a while. Urvashi would throw a tantrum. Laila had come to know her tirade by heart, even in such a short time.

"You don't care for me, Laila."

"I hate this country. There's *nothing* to do."

"My brother is such a pain, not that my sister is any better."

"I miss Cape Town. It's a buzzing city."

"Why is your mother so mean? Can't I come round just for a while?"

"My parents had another one of their arguments. I hate them."

Her laments had no end.

If Laila was honest, she would have to admit that Lakshmi was right—and so were the other girls in her class. They were constantly demanding to know how she could be friends with Urvashi. The question was posed on the rare occasions when Laila was alone.

Initially, the girls had tried to welcome her to a new school and country, but she had snubbed all offers of friendship. She was moody and grumpy. Sulky, most of the time. She never contributed in any class and spoke to no one except Laila. Laila was proud that the new foreign student had picked her for a friend, that she deigned to talk to her.

"How can you talk to Urvashi?" What's wrong with you Laila?" Esther would demand every Monday morning at assembly.

"Miss Bipolar" would be on everyone's lips as they nudged each other. Like a game of Chinese whispers.

As the friendship thickened, Laila's other friends barely spoke to her. Her popularity had waned; they avoided her like the plague. Even Zoe had confronted her about it, even though they had drifted apart since the incident with her father.

"Urvashi is using you, Laila. Be careful," she'd said while they walked between classes.

Janet, who had sat beside Laila through seven years of primary school and three years of secondary, now no longer even looked at her. They had been as thick as thieves before Urvashi's arrival.

"She'll hurt you, Laila. Don't say I didn't warn you." Janet had pulled Laila into the girl's toilet, making her declaration back when they'd still talked to each other.

Laila shrugged Janet's hand off her shoulder. "Who made you my mother? I don't need your warning. Just leave me alone."

"Don't come crawling back to me." Janet's golden eyes flashed angrily. Were those tears Laila spotted behind the fierce demeanour?

"I won't. Bye-bye."

Good riddance, Laila thought. Then why did she feel like sobbing? She missed the laughter she'd shared with Janet. The way they sang "Do You Think I'm Sexy" by Rod Steward or "Another Brick in the Wall" by Pink Floyd at the top of their voices at break time. The juicy mangoes sprinkled with chilli powder Janet shared with her after lunch. The long walks they took on the hockey field, arm in arm. The crazy 'knock-knock' jokes Janet made up. The way Janet braided Laila's hair during maths class.

"Push your chair back, Laila, my hands can't reach your hair," Janet would whisper. With outstretched arms, she would make tiny braids at the nape of

53

Laila's neck, under the oblivious eye of Mr Kimani, the lanky teacher who had a passion for red and green velvet sweaters and throwing bits of chalk at unsuspecting girls when their concentration dwindled, which was often in Laila's case.

Laila put down their reaction to jealousy. That explained their resentment. It was the reason why they wanted her to cull her friendship with Urvashi.

But Laila knew that not all the girls in school could be jealous. If she was honest, she would have to agree that Urvashi was demanding as a friend.

What was the hold Urvashi had over her?

Urvashi was no bright spark. Admittedly, her stories were grandiose. The places she had been to. The friends she had in Cape Town. Her numerous trips to Geneva, London, Milan, and New York.

"At mid-term we're going to Geneva. I love it there. The Swiss are the loveliest people and the shopping is a-maz-ing." Her oval face would come alive when she described her adventures. The people she had met, the sights she had seen. The places she would go on the next holiday. Fascinating tales. Stories far removed from Laila's ordinary world.

The only place Laila had ever been was Malindi on the Kenyan coast, every August for two weeks. The eight-hour road journey couldn't compare to the flights Urvashi took several times in a year. She spoke about Alitalia, Air France, Swiss Air and KLM like old friends, even boasting of sitting with the pilot in the cockpit. A flight to Malindi would have been out of the question for the Cardoso family. Lakshmi would never spend hard-earned money on such an extravagance.

Laila couldn't even think of another girl in her class who had flown.

54

Was Laila infatuated with Urvashi? Maybe in love with her? Her life was so *interesting* in comparison.

Urvashi's family was exotic. Actors in a fascinating family saga like *Dallas* or *Dynasty*. Far removed from Laila's lacklustre family.

Her mother drove a sleek silver Mercedes, and her father had a bright crimson BMW. Flashy cars! Amit drove a battered green Peugeot 404 while Lakshmi didn't even know how to drive.

Whenever Meera, Urvashi's mother, picked her and her older sister and brother up from school, she was elegantly dressed. Her silk saris were flamboyant and fashionable with sequins and sparkles. Colourful bangles adorned her wrists and pearl chokers her neck. Earrings dangled from dainty earlobes. Her high-heeled silver or gold sandals clattered as she walked. Her makeup complemented the colour of her sari, as did her *bindi*. Purple, green or blue eyeshadow, lashes thick with mascara, and blusher on high cheekbones. A fiery red mouth that pouted petulantly, like a model in the glossy magazines. Her hair was immaculately blow-dried, the ringlets falling perfectly to her shoulders. The perfumes she wore left a trail of heady aroma like a blanket, suffocating but at the same time comforting.

Laila was in awe of Meera. Her coquettish ways. Perfectly manicured slim fingers held her cigarette in a black lacquer holder, a mysterious, hazy aura of smoke swirling around her. She could have easily walked off the set of *Casablanca*. Her expensive clothes and shoes. Her jet-setting lifestyle. Her lazy drawl when she spoke Italian to impress them. Her *je ne sais quoi*!

Why couldn't Lakshmi be more like Meera?

Lakshmi, who owned one bottle of perfume, Coty, which she used sparingly on Sundays. Lakshmi, who possessed one lipstick. When it was used up, she scraped the bottom out with her index finger before buying a new tube. Lakshmi, who wore her only pair of high heels on Sundays to mass. Lakshmi, whose wardrobe boasted cotton skirts, polyester blouses and boring African-print kaftan dresses. Lakshmi, who frequented the school of hairdressing for her haircuts—no shampoo, just the cut and no blow-dry. Lakshmi, who lavished Laila with love, kisses and cuddles that Laila squirmed to get away from.

"Why don't we have a cook?" Laila had demanded. "Urvashi has one. They even have a chauffeur and a gardener. They have two maids."

"Well, Laila, they have more money. Don't you prefer my food to that of a cook?" Lakshmi asked kindly. Every meal was whipped up with love, no matter how tiring her day at work had been.

Lakshmi, who was all ears every evening when Laila narrated her school day. Lakshmi, who dedicated weekends to Laila and Tamer. Lakshmi, who didn't take off on a plane every three months because she needed a break from her family. Lakshmi, who sang Laila to sleep every evening. Lakshmi, who hand-made Laila her favourite meals. Lakshmi, who brushed and braided Laila's thick ebony hair every morning before she left for school and again in the evening before she tucked her into bed. Lakshmi, who gave Laila head massages every Saturday, leaving her hair black and glossy with coconut oil. Lakshmi, who sat with Laila at the dining table every weekday to ensure her homework was done.

Sitting cross-legged on her narrow bed, Laila wondered why everyone disliked Urvashi. Could there be some truth in what they said? She refused to question herself too deeply, afraid of the truth. She ignored the warning bells that jangled loudly in her head.

Still, she wouldn't give up Urvashi. She was a drug, and Laila had become addicted. She didn't fathom that with any drug there would be side effects and withdrawal symptoms. That didn't bear thinking about. Not now. Not ever.

"Can I come over to your house today? Please?" Urvashi used her puppy-dog eyes. She stuck her lower lip out, pouting. It had been over two weeks since her last visit, and Laila was still not on talking terms with Lakshmi. The bare necessities, just to be civil.

Amit had only yesterday asked her to be nicer to her mother. She was hurting.

"I hate her," Laila had told him through gritted teeth.

Was that anger or sadness in her father's eyes? "Don't talk like that about your mother, Laila. What's wrong with you? This is not the way we've brought you up."

Laila knew better than to answer back. She would never dare. She was too afraid of him. She loved him too much. Her love bordered on worship. Her father was handsome and muscular. He had wavy jet-black hair and a perfect pencil moustache. He looked like Rock Hudson, the Indian version.

When he played football with his work colleagues every weekend, Laila thought he looked like a Greek god with his six-pack and bulging calf muscles, in his blue shorts and white vest. Her heart would swell with pride. He was cool compared to the other dads, who sported big paunches, bushy eyebrows and balding heads—the likes of Mr Fernando.

Amit never denied her anything. Lakshmi didn't know that every week he gave her one shilling to buy glucose sweets. He bought her presents for her birthday and Christmas. They watched Scooby-Doo at 6:00 p.m. every evening, sitting side by side. She laughed or smirked only when Amit did. She mimicked his every gesture when eating and drinking. He was her hero.

"Your mother is right, you know, about your friend."

Her father too, Laila thought. He had never mentioned Urvashi. He had always been pleasant to her. But he was in cahoots with the rest of them. Laila felt bereft.

"You're misjudging her, Daddy. She really is nice." Laila tried to put some calm in her voice, which was sounding whiny to her own ears. Could she really not see clearly? Could they all be wrong about the same person?

"No, Laila, it's *you* who are misjudging her." Amit stared sadly at Laila, his ebony eyes glassy with unshed tears. "You care more for this girl than your own family. Invite her back into our home. I don't want to see your mother upset. I'll talk to her."

With that, he strode off to read the *Daily Nation*. Laila was over the moon. She had won.

Urvashi sauntered back into their home quicker than a bullet that had missed the heart. Instead of killing her target on impact, she made sure her victims bled slowly and painfully.

She openly snubbed Lakshmi, whom she wouldn't even deign to greet, though she practically lived with them. She was there every day after school, helping herself to food from the kitchen and drinks from the fridge.

"Who should we call today?" Urvashi said. She flipped through the telephone directory before picking up the black telephone.

Laila stared in shock. No one in the Cardoso house was allowed to use the phone without Lakshmi's permission. How could Urvashi use it to make prank calls, bold as brass? Laila cringed in fear of her mother's wrath.

Lakshmi never commented on Urvashi's lack of manners or her obnoxious behaviour, but Laila could feel her mother bite her tongue. It was a wonder with Urvashi sorely frustrating her that she hadn't bitten it off completely! Laila supposed she accepted Urvashi in her house for the sake of peace and sanity, her love for Laila boundless.

Laila wouldn't give up Urvashi. She was her best friend, even when she threw horrific tantrums. She had a foul temper, ranting when she didn't get her way. Lashing out verbally. At such times Laila wished she could put a muzzle on her, but when she was in a good mood, Laila beamed. Urvashi would be kind and considerate, smiling and laughing—a rarity but worth all the woe Laila put up with. Urvashi was like a good actor. Laila never knew when the acting stopped and reality started.

Several months later, Lakshmi tried to reason with Laila late one Sunday evening. "Friends like Urvashi will only bring you down, my child. Listen to your mother. I say this for your own good."

Urvashi had spent the entire Sunday with the Cardosos. Her mood had been horrendous. She had sat at the dining table but refused to eat a morsel of food. She had shuffled her feet irritatingly, even though Amit had asked her quietly to sit still. She stared glumly at the floor or the ceiling, sighing loudly or rolling her eyes in exaggerated boredom.

"What funny food you eat. My mother only buys us fillet steak, and we *only* eat basmati rice."

How could she be so insensitive? Laila thought when she saw Lakshmi's face turn the colour of beetroot. Amit's eyes threw daggers in Laila's direction, but he had held his tongue.

"This meat looks like my gardener's shoe sole," Urvashi said, lifting the slice of rump steak with the edge of her fork.

"Lucky us, having the pleasure of eating your gardener's shoe sole!" Lakshmi retorted without missing a beat. It was Urvashi who turned beetroot, then.

"There's no need to demean people," Lakshmi added quietly. "You won't find fillet steak in my house, Urvashi, so please feel free to call your mother to pick you up."

Urvashi had ignored the request, preferring to torture everyone with her behaviour. Tamer had kicked Laila twice, mouthing that Urvashi should leave. She stubbornly sat at the table, ruining the meal for the rest of them.

It had been a taxing day, even for Laila. Now Lakshmi was having a go at her about her friendship. It fell on deaf ears. She walked out of the sitting room pretending she hadn't heard her mother. Lakshmi stopped trying.

Urvashi knew how to hurt Laila. For no reason, she would stop talking to her. She would laugh and joke with the other girls like they were her best friends. Draping her arms around the shoulder of Zoe, Mita or Beatrice. She wouldn't have dared try that on Janet, who would have never put up with such hypocrisy.

"Who wants Swiss chocolates?"

Urvashi passed bars of chocolates to whomever would accept them in the class, purposely ignoring Laila.

"Take one." Mita nudged Gladys. "It's our lucky day."

The girls went with the flow of Urvashi's mood swings, throwing knowing looks in Laila's direction.

Tears stung Laila's eyes, and rage clouded her good sense. How she would have loved to throttle Urvashi.

Then a few days later, Urvashi would kiss Laila loudly on both cheeks, enveloping her in a bear hug.

"I've missed you, Laila. Why haven't you spoken to me for the last three days?"

Laila would stare dumbfounded at Urvashi. Things would go back to normal until the next time Urvashi got tired of Laila and deemed she needed space, relegating Laila to a cold corner as her time out. Each time, Laila foolishly picked up the friendship from where they'd left off, forgiving Urvashi for her ridiculous behaviour.

Urvashi was like snot that refused to be flicked off. If she couldn't come over or wasn't getting enough attention, she would threaten Laila with the use of her favourite phrase.

"If I can't come to your house this weekend, I'll kill myself." Green eyes flashed angrily, nostrils flaring.

Laila was scared. In the beginning, she'd thought this was just the idle threat of a teenage girl starved for attention. Slowly, she began to live in fear. Fear of the ever-increasing tantrums. Fear of how far things could escalate with the slightest provocation.

After an argument, Laila would lie on her bed plotting her revenge. Elaborate schemes for how she would get rid of Urvashi. Her imaginings bordered on murder.

Laila feared she was turning into a monster. Some days, she hardly recognised herself.

She was caught in Urvashi's clutches.

Then Urvashi had made good on her threat and slashed her wrists. She'd been rushed to Hospital. Since then, her family and especially Laila had walked on eggshells. Laila hadn't dared tell her parents when Meera had given her the news outside the school gate.

"Urvashi was rushed last night to Hospital," Meera had said. She wasn't her flamboyant self. Her hair was loosely knotted at the nape of her neck. Sweaty stray tendrils clung to her forehead. Makeup free, she wore a crumpled kaftan instead of a silk sari and *chappals*.

"Why?" Laila squeaked, knowing the reason before Meera's answer.

The wisdom of Lakshmi's words was coming to pass.

The addictive friendship continued for several years. Laila tried to quit, but each time Urvashi roiled up such havoc that Laila gave in, a bit of herself dying in the toxic relationship. Laila had to keep a tight check on her anger, not wanting to turn into a clone of Urvashi.

"Where has my happy-go-lucky-Laila disappeared to?" Lakshmi asked, trying to envelop Laila in a bear hug.

Laila slipped out of her mother's grasp. The calm, placid, happy girl was nowhere to be found.

It seemed to Laila that Urvashi's family were only too happy not to have her at home. The more time she spent with Laila, the better for them. The attempted suicide was swept under the carpet.

Let the Cardosos deal with their choleric daughter.

Meera never hugged nor kissed her children. The presents and holidays made up for the lack of love. Her time was spent in Italy, Spain and Barbados with friends.

The characters who had enthralled Laila had flaws. The glamour was wearing off, and the captivating saga was turning into a horror movie.

Once strong, determined and independent, Laila was weak in Urvashi's company. She didn't recognise the person she was becoming, a sulky, morose teenager who cried alone in her room, afraid of the changes in her comportment and the effects Urvashi had on her.

Dating Kurt was a feat in itself. If Urvashi had been jealous before of sharing Laila, now her possessiveness grew a hundredfold. She would have fits of jealous rage. Hours later, she would plead for forgiveness, but still she demanded that Laila spend more time with her. How dare Laila find love!

Laila was suffocating. How could she juggle her love life and this toxic relationship successfully? She felt like her head was on a guillotine and would be chopped off at the smallest provocation.

She wasn't in contact with any school friends. They had drifted away. Laila longed to confide in Janet. Or talk to Usha or Esther. Normal girls. Normal friends. She had only herself to blame. Hadn't she given them the cold shoulder to start with? *We told you so* would be too much to bear.

Laila tried to break free from Urvashi's shackles, but each time the threat was waved like a magic wand. Did she want Urvashi's suicide on her conscience, however much she wanted to be rid of her?

Tears were ever at the ready with her. They would gush out at the drop of a hat, abating as soon as she got her way. Laila questioned her sanity. Was she going bonkers? She felt claustrophobic in Urvashi's company.

The fascinating stories had curdled with the years. No longer were they awe-inspiring, or impressive. Now they sounded like the fabrications of an over-active imagination of a girl desperate for attention.

Laila needed space. Breath. *Deep breaths*, she would tell herself when they were together.

The friendship was becoming poisonous. Laila wanted to hit Urvashi. She dreamt of killing her. She wanted to run away. She wanted her freedom.

Lakshmi was gallingly right! So were all her school friends; so was Amit. How could she have been so stupid? Laila berated herself often for her naiveté. She was a puppet, and Urvashi kept on deftly pulling her strings.

After her marriage to Kurt, Laila began to use her husband as an excuse for Urvashi not to come over. "We have a dinner invitation this evening," or "Kurt needs to work from the apartment." These phrases had no effect on Urvashi's hippo hide. They only made things worse.

She would be there religiously every morning and evening. All weekends. She demanded room service, used the hotel swimming pool and parking facilities.

There was no end to her manipulation.

The births of Lili and Lalita made things worse. She began coming in the afternoons on the pretext of playing with the babies.

"Why does she have to be a constant fixture in our lives?" Kurt asked, exasperated. "Looks like she's part of the furniture and fittings of the hotel."

Laila would cajole him with, "She needs me." "Give her time." "Her bark is worse than her bite."

Why was she defending Urvashi's obnoxious behaviour to Kurt? Why was she putting her marriage in jeopardy?

He was a saint and reminded Laila of how much Lakshmi had put up with. She realised too late the living hell life had been for her mother with Urvashi's constant presence in their lives while growing up. Her mother had suffered in silence. Her love for her daughter knew no bounds.

Laila wanted to protect her precious Lili and Lalita from making similar friendships in the future. But how, when she tightened the noose daily around her own neck?

Why hadn't she heeded the advice that everyone freely gave her at the beginning? Why hadn't she seen through Urvashi the way they had?

Finally, Urvashi fell in love.

Laila was thrilled. She thanked the good Lord for his intervention. The noose loosened. Urvashi was wrapped up with her beau, visits to the hotel apartment dwindled, and Laila found time to spend alone with her family. Bliss.

Then the tables turned.

With her love life flourishing, Urvashi wanted nothing to do with Laila. Wasn't this what Laila had longed for, for years? Freedom? Laila had spent her teenage and early married years dancing to Urvashi's tune. The music had stopped playing.

At the wedding, Laila was ignored in favour of Urvashi's husband's family and friends, who took themselves and their titles too seriously.

"They've come all the way from New York." New York wasn't in another galaxy. People zipped there for the weekend.

"What's so great about New York?" Laila wanted to ask.

Ameer, Urvashi's husband, rattled off his likes and dislikes. His wonderful family, their acceptance of her. The expensive restaurants they frequented, the designer clothes she bought, the spa treatments, the money they spent, the bottled water they drank—unlike the rest of the Kenyan population, who boiled water! The list was long, and Laila was no longer listening. The stories were monotonous and pretentious. Ameer was God's gift to women-kind.

Love is blind.

"You know, you should address Ameer as 'Doctor' when you speak to him."

Laila stared at Urvashi like she had lost her mind. Had she heard right? Was she pulling her leg? Urvashi was serious.

Laila laughed mirthlessly. "You got to be kidding me, Urvashi."

"Well, he is a doctor, after all."

"And I'm not a patient, after all!"

The cheek. How dare she. Seven years married to Kurt, and Urvashi had treated their home as a pit stop for food and drink and hotel entertainment in the form of music recitals, theme buffets and functions. Why was she throwing titles in Laila's direction? Really, shouldn't she address Kurt as "General

Manager"? "Saint" would be more appropriate, considering all he had put up with!

"What are you wearing, Laila? Aren't those trousers too big?"

"Why don't you wear more makeup? You're so boring with only lipstick."

"Paint your toenails, for heaven's sake!"

Who made her the fashion police? Had Joan Rivers employed her as a personal assistant?

Laila lay low, revelling in her new-found freedom. Lakshmi never threw the famous *I told you so* at her daughter. She did give her knowing looks whenever calls were ignored and rendezvous cancelled.

The breaking point came when Urvashi had her first child. Laila decided to stop by one sunny afternoon for a chat, maybe a cup of tea. Their friendship, if you could call it that, went back a while, after all. She'd brought a present, a soft toy elaborately wrapped by the salesgirl in the Mothercare shop.

"Leave it on the table," Urvashi said dismissively. "I wish you had called first. This isn't a good time for me."

It had always been a good time for you to walk in and out of my mother's house. I had no weekdays nor weekends free with my husband or my children.

Urvashi had forgotten how she had barged into Laila's life every day of the week—public holidays, Christmas, Easter and New Year included. Laila had allowed her to play with her daughters, accepted her mood swings and sulks. Her outbursts of temper and her tantrums.

These accusations went through Laila's mind. She wanted to strike her. Gouge her eyes out and spit at her. A few choice abuses went through her mind.

Instead, Laila walked slowly to the front door. She turned at the sound of Urvashi's voice crooning to her baby in the cradle.

"What a loser she turned out to be," she was saying. "She'll never amount to much. She's too stupid. You and I, my child, have places to go. We have better things to do than hang around people like her."

Laila couldn't believe her ears.

Instead of the fury that was roiling up a few seconds ago, she felt a calm settle over her. Peace she hadn't felt in a long time. Laila smiled. A wide smile. A smile of relief. She had her key to freedom. The torment would come to an end. Finally. She would walk out and never look back.

Realisation had dawned, and with it, the possibility that perhaps Urvashi was not and had never been mentally stable. Since her marriage, she had changed. Her mannerisms and speech were calmer, condescending. Could anyone have changed so drastically? Did Ameer know the manipulative side of his wife? The moody side?

Did she need professional help? Laila wondered. Or could love cure her of her volatile behaviour?

Laila knew she'd deserved what she'd got. She had put Urvashi first instead of her family. Urvashi had crept into her life. Like dreadlocks, she had entwined her tendrils around Laila. She no longer needed Laila. Shaving off the dreadlocks was the easiest option. Urvashi wanted her new life to be as smooth as a bald head.

She would have it. Laila's smile broke into a grin. Urvashi didn't realise the favour she was doing her. Without a backward look, she strode out of the house. Life had just got better. This time, she would keep the door to her family firmly locked from Urvashi. She would throw away the key.

***

February 2005

Laila was slumped on the rickety bamboo chair. The February sun warmed her face and shoulders. Fluffy cumulus clouds raced across the sky. Colourful bedsheets, towels and an assortment of clothes flapped in the warm afternoon wind. A row of sparrows lined the rooftop, twittering excitedly. She could hear Mrs Gupta shouting at her maid for burning a sari.

"*Samahani memsaab. Pole sana.*" Fervent apologies were repeated over and over.

"I'll cut your salary at the end of the month, Marylin. Last week you broke a plate *and* a glass. Aie. I'm not made of money, Mama."

Laila could clearly envision the finger-wagging that went with Mrs Gupta's idle threats. Marylin had raised Daljit and Hema, Mrs Gupta's two girls, as her own. She could prepare an *allou* and *bindi* curry, potatoes and lady-fingers better than her memsaab, or knead the dough for chapattis in a flash. She lovingly tended to the dhania, parsley, mint and curry leaf tree in the tiny garden patch as well as the jasmine creeper that enveloped the vicinity with its heady aroma. She raised her hands in adoration whenever she passed by Lord Ganesha in the prayer area of the Gupta household, the way she had observed the family do over the years. Every morning, she placed a fresh marigold on the altar as her offering.

"Remove obstacles in our way, Lord," Marylin would pray.

Marylin had worked for Sangeeta Gupta for as long as Laila could remember. She was family.

The wall that separated the Guptas' house from the Cardosos' wasn't very high. Life unfolded on a daily basis between the two families like the rhythm of a train on iron tracks—reassuring and comforting. Neighbourly. The goings-on between the two families for the last twenty years had been mundane. The washing of clothes, the banter, the weekly frying of samosas or bhajis outside to eliminate food odours in the house. Food was regularly handed over the wall by both Sangeeta and Lakshmi. Long conversation took place while both women carried out their chores. Trays of Diwali and Christmas sweets were anticipated, tasted and enjoyed by two culinary critics. Lifts into town when a car broke down, or a bowl of sugar, rice or eggs when either ran out. Vegetarian meals that Sangeeta avidly taught Lakshmi. Mango, lime, aubergine or gherkin pickles that Lakshmi taught Sangeeta in turn.

Laila smiled tiredly. It had been two weeks since Lakshmi's cremation. Two weeks that had flown by with all the sorting Laila had done. It had been heartbreaking rifling through her mother's things. Cupboards of clothes and jewellery. Lakshmi's familiar smell wafted through everything, often bringing tears to Laila's eyes.

How she missed her mother.

She found drawers full of every card or letter Laila or Tamer had sent over the years. It was hard throwing memories away. Clothes and shoes were bagged and given away to the needy, and eventually, the cupboards were clean and bare. With Lakshmi's belongings gone, so was her lingering perfume. Amit had sat in front of the open doors, sobbing.

It was heart-wrenching, closing a chapter in a loved one's life, but it had to be done. Over seventy years had been given away, but Lakshmi would remain in their hearts and heads.

"Mama, there's someone to see you at the gate. Shall I let her in?" Njeri, the maid, asked. Her coffee-coloured skin glowed.

Njeri had started working a year ago for the Cardoso family. Angela, who had worked for them for thirty years, had gone back home to Kisumu. At sixty-one years old, she had needed her retirement, but Laila was sure she hadn't been able to bear seeing Lakshmi deteriorate before her eyes.

Who, Laila wondered, wanted to see her? She nodded wearily to Njeri to let the visitor in. This was probably another condolence visit.

Laila stared in utter bafflement at Urvashi. The extra kilos didn't suit her. Her eyes were puffy and over-made-up. Her thinning hair fell limply to her shoulders.

"I read in the newspapers that your mum passed away. I wanted to come sooner." Urvashi stood awkwardly, a half-smile on her thin mouth.

Laila tried to compose all the feelings coursing through her veins. Anger at the top.

Urvashi bent to place a kiss on Laila's cheek. Laila moved from her slouching position to an upright one, thus evading the Judas kiss.

"Tamer texted me that you were still in town."

Tamer, as ever, comfortable on enemy ground, Laila thought. He had spent two days after the funeral leaving Laila, as usual, to handle things, but had found time to text Urvashi!

"I'm so sorry," Urvashi said. "I know that Lakshmi meant the world to you, Laila. I cared for her too."

Laila wanted to burst out laughing. Urvashi cared for Lakshmi? After the torment she had caused her mother for years? Had she forgotten her insolence? Her obnoxious behaviour? She had been nothing but a thorn in Lakshmi's side.

The "thank you" came out drily. This was the last straw. Laila couldn't deal with Urvashi, not when she had just lost her mother. Urvashi dragged over the stool that was in the corner, settling her large hips on it.

"I don't know what happened between us, Laila. I've tried to contact you for years, but you're not on social media. Why did you stop keeping in touch? Why didn't you let me know when you left Nairobi for Saudi Arabia? Tamer told me."

Did Tamer have verbal diarrhoea?

"I've lost all my childhood memories. I tried to get in touch with you to fill in the blanks, but it was like searching for a needle in a haystack. I know that we were close, but besides that, I don't have any recollection of my adolescence."

Laila stared at Urvashi in amazement. Was she hearing right? Did she have the audacity to use amnesia as an excuse for her behaviour?

Is that what the doctor has diagnosed or her own conclusions? Was she her husband's patient? Laila didn't voice her thoughts. She wasn't going down that road. Some things are better left in the past.

"I just draw a blank when I think of my teenage years." Urvashi shrugged. The awkwardness was back. Tears filled her eyes, and she turned to brush them away. "All I ask is for your forgiveness, Laila. Please."

Forgiveness.

Could she forgive? Laila wondered absently.

"Can't we be friends again?"

No, they couldn't be friends again. That was certain.

But she would forgive Urvashi. Life was too short. She probably had paid her dues living with the guilt all these years. Maybe she had lost her memory. Laila would give her the benefit of the doubt.

Laila smiled sadly. They had both changed. Life had meandered its way, and after all these years, their paths had crossed again. Why hold a grudge? The wound had been deep, but it was no longer festering. She could deal with the scar that would remain.

"I forgive you, Urvashi. Really, I do. However, our lives are different. I don't think we have anything in common anymore."

"Can't we be friends?" A subtle whine crept into Urvashi's voice.

"I don't think so."

"I'm truly sorry about your mum."

"I know. Thank you."

It was an apology for all the years that she had hurt Lakshmi. Laila would accept it on behalf of her mother.

"I'm sorry too about the past. You know, our childhood and everything." Urvashi waved her hand distractedly.

Laila wanted to point out that she had supposedly lost her memory, but held back. "I know."

"Can I come back to see you? I have four children. I'd like you to meet them. Did you have any more children after Lili and Lalita?"

Laila shook her head.

"Can I come back to see you?" Urvashi repeated her question.

"Maybe before I leave. I'm here for another three weeks."

"Thank you, Laila." She kissed Laila on her cheek. This time, Laila didn't move away.

Would she see Urvashi again? She didn't know. It was too soon to make a decision. She would, however, let go of the past.

CHAPTER 4

"ONE DAY"

September 1984

Laila had never dreamt of being a princess like other little girls. She felt she already was. Perhaps in her last life, she had been one. She remembered how she would come down the stairs as a child, one hand on the banister, taking one dainty step after another.

In her dreams, she didn't live in a palace but a hotel. It was luxurious and lavish. Plush. The excitement of stepping into a lobby with thick carpets and glittering chandeliers, where the cutlery shone and the glassware twinkled. Where tablecloths were impeccably pressed. Where waiters placed a linen napkin on a lap and whisked away an empty plate. Where a bed was turned down in the evenings and the curtains drawn shut. Where a warm bath was run with red rose petals floating in the water and scented candles flickered, drawing long shadows in a cosy interior. Divine. Where fluffy towels hung on a heating rail ready to enfold a damp body in warmth. Where laundry could be left in a bag and would be returned with missing buttons sewn back on, attire perfectly pressed and hung in a wardrobe, or a suitcase unpacked and clothes neatly folded away by a butler after a long flight. Where shoes were shone and neatly tied in a shoe bag to keep away dust. Where mouth-watering dishes were the press of a button away any time of day or night.

It was a wide-eyed world filled with wonder for fourteen-year-old Laila. It smelt of prestige and fame, of luxury in every sense of heady comfort.

"Laila, come help me in the kitchen," Lakshmi said.

"I helped you yesterday. Why do I need to help you *again* today?" Laila replied petulantly.

"When you have your own house, you won't choose the days you want to work, my child."

"I'll never work, Mummy. I'll live in a hotel."

"Right now, you're living in my house. Come and help me." Lakshmi laughed. "Remember your poor mother when you live in a grand hotel."

Laila shut her eyes, imagining herself in a hotel far away. Sheer curtains billowed in the wind. Bay windows were left wide open to a breathtaking vista of azure seas and rolling mountains in the distance. Pink, white and fuchsia oleander bushes dotted the view, and pine trees stood tall like sentinels.

Just wait, Laila thought. I will *live in a hotel. I'll never have to clean or cook, do laundry or the dishes.*

Dreams do come true.

She met Kurt while temping for six months at a five-star hotel in Nairobi. She had filled in for the personal assistant to the general manager, who had gone abroad on training.

"Can I tempt you to have coffee with me today?" Kurt's blue eyes twinkled.

"I'm busy today," Laila had replied flatly.

"Dinner? Lunch? Breakfast? Are you free this week?"

"Busy. Don't even have time for tea." Laila tried to hide her smile.

The more abrupt she was with Kurt, the harder he dogged her on going on a date.

Finally, Laila conceded. "I'm free for lunch on Friday."

One date had led to another, and then another, until she was falling head over heels.

The tricky bit had been explaining a white man to Amit. Lakshmi was the go-between, explaining to Laila's father that times were changing and that strong-headed Laila would never agree to an arranged marriage. Laila had sat on pins, desperately wanting not only her father's approval but his acceptance of Kurt as well.

The courting began. Kurt would arrive every Sunday at the Cardoso household, impeccably dressed, a bottle of wine or whisky for Amit and flowers for Lakshmi. This gesture put him on a pedestal in Lakshmi's eyes; Amit never offered her flowers.

"What a beautiful bouquet, Kurt." Lakshmi was flattered. "Thank you."

"You're more than welcome, Lakshmi!" Kurt said with aplomb.

"Have you seen my flowers, Amit?" She waltzed in the kitchen with the bunch of pink roses.

Kurt discussed football and the global political situation, both passionate subjects for Amit. He complimented Lakshmi on her cuisine, to the extent of exchanging recipes. He showed them respect and love. He wooed Laila's parents the way he had their daughter in a most gentlemanly way.

Grudgingly, Amit had given in.

Living in a hotel had many princess-like attributes. She had room service whenever she didn't have the urge to whip up a meal, housekeeping that provided clean white sheets and towels on a daily basis, laundry, pressing and dry-cleaning services. Speciality restaurants, a chauffeur driven-car and spa treatments were perks provided in her modest five-star world.

Seven-star hotels, the likes of Burj Al-Arab, were sprouting like mushrooms around the globe, each more prestigious than the one before. Classy hotels where the receptionist wasn't picking her nose during check-in, and there wasn't kinky hair imbedded in bath towels!

Why stay at a five-star hotel, when you could splurge on a private butler and helicopter, where the linen was Egyptian virgin cotton of the finest quality or silk sheets if need be? Bath towels were bath sheets, wrapping two comfortably! A two-hundred-dollar white truffle omelette for breakfast and bathing in champagne bubbles or milk, like Cleopatra, were part of the exclusive services. A pillow and duvet menu were part of the bedside literature! Lavender vaporisers were perfectly placed on a plumped pillow at turn-down to lull guests to sleep, or ginger and cucumber by the desk to revitalise and boost lagging energy levels. An espresso machine a la George Clooney—what else? Oolong and Bergamot tea leaves handpicked from the finest plantations, complimentary. Gorgeous floral arrangements in lobbies almost meriting a landscaper.

An in-room masseuse and personal trainer were a phone call away; personalised bed and bath linen and stationary added attention to detail. The guest's favourite flowers, from hydrangeas to peonies to lilies to gardenias, elaborately arranged in a crystal vase, standing to attention in the suite. A concierge to provide the sold-out Beyoncé or Coldplay concert tickets or the Real Madrid versus Arsenal match. A private lift to whisk the incognito celebrity to the penthouse suite. Or an escort for a day or three, billed under room service order, a discreet service provided to discerning clientele.

But Laila thrived in the five-star world. She was comfortable in this milieu. Sitting in a hotel lobby was fascinating. The coming and going of people of various nationalities, be they business people or illicit lovers, honeymooners or excited families. Long-staying guests, celebrities or passers-by who want to get out of the cold and the rain or scorching heat all walked through the same revolving doors, the doorman ready to doff his hat slightly or laboriously, depending on the status of the guest. The lower the gesture, the higher the tip.

Her life wasn't as glamorous as that of Paris Hilton or as privileged. After all, she was just the wife of the general manager. Nor was it as gruesome as in Stephen King's *The Shining*, though some of the people she met during her travels were like characters out of the movie; weird! Others were even likeable. It took all sorts to make the world. Lakshmi often said that all five fingers are not the same.

Egos were big.

"Look!" Laila whispered to Kurt.

The commotion in the lobby between the star and the porters was hilarious. Latex gloves were produced by the personal assistant and distributed. "Don't you dare touch any item of luggage without gloves!"

"Does she whip out gloves for luggage handlers at the airport?" Kurt commented.

"Soufflé," Laila whispered. It was her code name for celebrities having a big head, nicely swollen but collapsing immediately when taken out! Laila shook her head, winking at her husband.

"I better take a look," Kurt said, striding off.

Women constantly vied for each other's attention, having a Nicki Minaj or Mariah Carey moment whenever they could. Proof that they were living it up better than their friends or enemies.

There is only one thing in life worse than being talked about, and that is not being talked about. Oscar Wilde had hit the nail on the head. The constant need to keep up with the Joneses, Kumars, N'gengas and Aikidos.

Feeling like a princess and actually being one were two different things. No matter how luxurious her life or her husband's title, Laila was an outsider. She had a wealth of knowledge of people and places, but her demeanour was often mistaken for snobbery. That was the way she held herself, the unshakeable feeling that she was of royal descent, if only in her imagination.

A stickler for perfection, she dressed impeccably. Haircuts were slotted into her agenda every six weeks, not a day later. She brushed her hair and buttered her lips every night before climbing into bed. She dedicated ten minutes every morning to her eyebrows, threading or plucking them into shape. She only left the house when every strand of her hair was in place, her teeth gleaming and her body moisturised from head to foot. Her clothes were carefully pressed and her shoes shone. Everything had to be carried out to military precision.

Many stars were only as impeccable on the Red Carpet!

She cringed when she encountered people in social circles—be they the wives of ambassadors or ambassadors themselves, CEOs or managing directors—with dandruff snowflakes on their shoulders, stray nose and ear hair, bad breath, cracked heels and unpolished shoes. She could smell unwashed hair a mile away. She kerbed her urge to whisk out miniature moisturisers for 'flour-mill walkers', people with white and dry skin on their feet, elbows and hands! Dirty, grimy spectacles made her shudder; what could be seen through the finger-marks? Chipped nail polish? One minute was all that was needed to have clean, polish-free nails.

Women labelled her 'high maintenance' behind her back. She took it as a compliment. High maintenance was better than no maintenance!

Laila was a perfectionist. And no one liked a perfectionist, she realised quickly, especially one who was a stickler for cleanliness. It only antagonised other women. But it was hard to change when she was set in her ways. Even as a child, she would handwash her only uniform every afternoon after school. When there wasn't enough sun to dry the uniform, she would wear it damp the next morning, letting it dry on her.

Aloofness helped Laila keep afloat in a world where money and status mattered to all her acquaintances. She had been hurt many times, and now caution won over company.

She didn't want to feel vulnerable.

Her good dress sense didn't win her friends, on the contrary. Laila didn't care. She had high standards. There had to be some hierarchy. They should know their place—and her place was certainly not at their place! Women were ready to rip each other to pieces over better class reports, sport results or party invitations that weren't forthcoming.

She chose the people she kept company with meticulously. She needed her privacy, guarding it like a jewelled vault. She abhorred loud people. Did the entire room need to know about their fantastic job, salary, vacation or sexual exploits? Why over-share?

Laila was naïve. The world wasn't as fair as she believed. Some people were only too glad when others failed in life. Many would gladly put a spoke in a wheel when the wheel was turning too smoothly. The good piano teachers, hairdressers or dentists were guarded secrets for some expats. Finding the right places to shop at without having to navigate labyrinths of malls, souks or open markets could be daunting. Laila had experienced the 'I don't know' or 'I really couldn't help you' over and over.

Was divulging a good address so difficult?

"Did Urmila give you her business card?" Gabrielle, the wife of the Italian ambassador to Kenya, asked Laila.

"Yes, I saw her dishing them out to everyone at the cocktail."

"She does that, dish out cards. Be careful, though—she has two sets: one with the right number and one that no one will ever get through."

"What do you mean?" Laila asked naively.

"Laila, don't be silly. If she likes you, she hands over the right card; if she doesn't, you get struck off her list with the wrong card. That way you can't get in touch with her."

Laila laughed. Urmila, the wife of the Indian high commissioner, really thought too highly of herself.

Handing out business cards had become trendy, and Laila noticed it more and more during her travels.

The higher the echelon, the more difficult it was to meet and keep true friends. Laila often wondered how the rich and famous made friends if it was so difficult at her rung of the ladder.

Women who plied the streets of Mumbai or Senegal selling their wares or commuting to work would laugh to hear of Laila's "hardship". But it was difficult all the same.

Laila didn't have a halo around her head or wings on her back, nor was she as tough as many of the women she met along her travels. Why were some women she encountered like pythons, eating their prey whole and alive?

"Dahlia is only my fourth-best friend," she heard a tiny brunette announce to the group of ladies in the hotel loo. "She won't mind me telling you about her affair with the brother of her husband's best friend."

"Really? Dahlia who goes to confession once a month?"

"That's why she goes to confession, silly!"

Laughter echoed as the clique discussed their absent friends.

"Did you see Lucille at the Japanese National Day reception?"

"My oh my, she was a walking billboard for Chanel. Those ghastly earrings, CHA and NEL. What was *that* about?"

"It was too, too much. The shoes, the top, the bag, the bracelets—and the cherry was indeed those earrings. Perhaps Chanel pays her."

"Coco wouldn't pay a *nut* to advertise for her!"

"Good one, Louise."

"Now, ladies, admit that y'all are just jealous that her husband earns much more than your husbands. She can afford CHA-NEL."

'Yeah right," the ladies answered in unison, and they burst into giggles.

Laila spent much of her time at orphanages or with local women. She visited prisons, schools and hospitals whenever she had time to spare. Bedsheets and towels no longer in use by the hotel but still in good condition were distributed to orphanages or community hospitals. Leftover toiletries were welcomed like gifts from the Magi. She avoided women's associations, preferring to go alone with her contribution. Many 'clubs' were cauldrons of women tearing each other to shreds under the cover of charity. Snide comments and vicious gossip were par on the agenda, and Any Other Business was usually everybody's business!

It was hard to keep friendships going, even under normal circumstances. With Kurt's job requiring them to move every two to three years, it was made even harder. Laila enjoyed meeting people. Inquisitive by nature, she was keen to learn the cultures of the people in the countries she lived in. Food intrigued her. Taste and texture was a way of getting closer to local people and a good conversation starter. Having to smile with a crunchy, grilled caterpillar or refrain from gagging over the lamb's eyes floating in a thick tomato sauce was a good ice-breaker. The dark trail of ants in the sugar bowl was vitamin D, as was explained to her when she hesitated with the teaspoon. Laila had mastered the art of swallowing food that was not of her palate. It would be rude not to sample food offered, no matter how different it was from one's usual diet.

Locals in any country were friendly and welcoming. Eagerly, they proudly showed off the landscape and artisanal products from stone sculptures to wooden carvings.

"Good price, beautiful things in my small shop. Come!" The tiny Thai girl followed Laila around the market.

"How much?" Laila asked, fingering the sandalwood fan and lacquered coconut shell bowl.

"I give local price, ma'am."

"Yes, local price. I'm not a tourist." Laila smiled.

Clay incense burners in the Middle East. Mahogany animals in Kenya. Malachite and amethyst beads in the Congo, and elaborate footstools and headrests in Western Africa. An array of precious stones—garnet, turquoise, jade, rubies, moonstone, amber, quartz and emeralds—in Zambia, colours so vivid it was like opening a tin of Quality Street. Scary masks to ward off evil spirits in Central Africa. Frankincense and oud resin drops in the Sultanate of Oman.

Prices in every market were always local. Haggling was part of the fun. No matter how much the vendor insisted they were losing, a profit was made!

Lush forests in the Congo smelled of damp red earth, musty in the sweet morning air. Sunbirds regal in kaleidoscope feathers. Thick fronds heaving with raindrops from the tropical storm of the night before. Grey and red African parrots squawking in the sky. Samburu women haggling over the price of the woollen blankets, colourful beadwork piled around long necks and heaving on earlobes, the rolling plains of the Serengeti in the distance, and Mount Kilimanjaro's snow-covered peak a postcard backdrop. Wildebeest, buffaloes, zebra, gazelles and kudus munching on the expanse of golden grass, oblivious to the good-natured bargaining of tourists and locals. The intricate wood ceiling of the souk in Oman that dated back to the twelfth century; spices and perfume blended in the humid air. Thick cardamom coffee drunk by shop-owners sitting on the doorstep of each shop.

There were many things she loved about travelling, but it was oddly lonely. Laila tried to brush off the nagging feeling of being shunned by social circles, with little success. Could she be imagining the subtle animosity that followed her from continent to continent?

Friendships, Laila came to notice on her travels, were often fickle and not as long-lasting as the movies, radio and books portrayed. Women were strange creatures, regardless of where they came from.

Were friendships stronger growing up and living in the same environment all one's life? Or were they as rare there as they were in the ever-changing expatriate world? Was she cynical? Laila mused. She was over-cautious? Discreet. Was it her experience with Mr Fernando or Urvashi that made her wary of getting too close? Was this why she was twice shy? Could this be the reason for the wide berth?

Or did she simply not fit in? An Indian woman in a world of film stars, presidents, royalty, the rich and famous, where ambassadors rubbed shoulders with company directors, CEOs and designers, Laila quickly learned that smiling and nodding—and nodding off—was appropriate conversation, agreeing with opinions even though her own were totally different was more agreeable than stony silence or nervous laughter. But Laila enjoyed being the devil's advocate. She could stand her ground in a heated discussion, revelling in the adrenaline rush. Depending on her mood, she could debate for or against the topic.

Being outspoken didn't bode well in these social circles. Men especially didn't want to deal with an opinionated woman.

Heated debates between Laila and Kurt on politics, the environment, human rights, cuisine and novels were held in the privacy of the hotel apartment. Laila was adept at goading her husband, who for the sake of sanity often conceded defeat. She had been the head debater in school for good reason: the joy of winning an argument.

Laila was smart, sophisticated, sporty and savvy. She enjoyed a good game of tennis, a leisurely walk on a golf course with a caddy, or horseback riding. She was a passionate Formula One fan.

"Laila, I said two steps left. *Left*," Mila, the Russian dance teacher, said for the third time.

Dancing was certainly not Laila's forte, but she loved it. She never missed the Tuesday classes.

Her real talent was in languages—an eyebrow-raiser with the Japanese and Chinese, who'd answer her enthusiastically amid large smiles and low bowing.

Laila lived by three rules. Good manners were indispensable; they maketh the person. Appearances mattered; you never know who you could bump into. And kindness shouldn't be mistaken for weakness.

Laila liked to treat people the way she expected to be treated. It didn't matter if you were a prince or a pauper.

Laila remembered making her way through an elegantly decorated ballroom during a black-tie affair for diplomats and corporate business people. She recognised many in the crowd. The heady scent of hyacinths and freesias was redolent in the air. She knew she looked good. Her long skirt fitted like a glove. Her hair fell in soft curls to her shoulders. She beamed as she walked, waving and smiling. Enjoying the evening. The elegant function was being hosted by her husband; she had every right to be the belle of the ball!

"Your skirt."

Laila stared at the stranger, who had her hand on her shoulder, shielding her, and realised her 'derriere' was on display. The hem of the lace skirt was tucked prettily into her black low-hip panties, exposing the full length of her leg and bum. Her panties hugged her taut bottom perfectly.

No wonder they were smiling back at her!

"Thank you!" Laila fleetingly touched the woman's hand.

Without batting an eyelid, she flashed a dazzling smile at the crowd. She thanked the lady again. With a flourish, she unwedged her skirt from her panty, overtly smoothing it down. Head held high, Laila had continued across the ballroom.

Diplomats, commoners, superstars—all of them came through the revolving doors of the hotel industry, and all of them had complaints.

Do you know who I am? *If they didn't know who they were, how were others to know*?

The service is terrible here. I know the general manager, restaurant manager, or someone else with manager incorporated into their title. *Was that a threat or mere tattle*?

The steak or burger was over- or under-cooked at the last mouthful. As was the hair found on the plate, bizarrely the same colour as the complainant's.

The champagne didn't have enough bubbles. The microscopic insect in the bathtub was reason enough for a complimentary room night. The temperature of the pool too cold or far too hot. The room service order took ages to arrive, warranting a free meal.

Yet no one volunteered the fact that bath towels and bathrobes had been packed away in suitcases. Or that ashtrays and flower vases had mysteriously disappeared. Paintings in five-star hotels were now fastened with screws to avoid theft.

Of course, there were genuine complaints as well.

Mundane ones, like rooms not ready at check-in or overbookings. Or more seriously, the shower head that fell on the guest's bald pate in Kinshasa, or the company director who'd left a prostitute asleep while he checked out in Lagos. She'd created a scene in the lobby demanding that the hotel settle the amount! Why hadn't she stuck to the adage 'no money, no honey'?

Or another incident, when the managing director of Henkel Uganda demanded to know who was snoring during his meeting. His face had turned beetroot as he glared around the table at his managers.

Accusing looks were exchanged, but no culprit was found. The meeting continued, and a short time later, two short snores were heard again.

"What the hell is going on here?" he shouted, banging on the table.

The managers burst into laughter as the purr of someone sound asleep continued. It certainly wasn't any of them! Lifting the tablecloth, the director started laughing.

He shook the waiter awake.

"This is not the place to take a nap, my friend. You were meant to set up the room and not fall asleep after."

Then there was the beauty therapist in Dubai who stole from guests' purses while they had a mask on their face. The conference participant in Kenya who packed items from the buffet in a bag and threw it over the balcony to his friend below, who was a deft catcher. The elderly gentleman in Angola who passed away in his room and had to be discreetly carried down the service stairs into the waiting ambulance at the back of the hotel. The protocol with the American embassy had been mind-boggling! It was a surprise that murder charges weren't brought against the hotel!

The broken-hearted lover who slashed her wrists in the bathtub after her boyfriend told her he was moving on without her. The utter shock for the housekeeping attendant in Ethiopia. Or the superstar who took all the bathroom fittings, including the gold-plated taps, soap dish, showerhead, light fixtures and grab rail, in Bahrain. Surely, those would look better in his Los Angeles mansion. Stars who required oxygen before a concert or interview as they were comatose on alcohol or drugs or both.

Credit card fraud in almost all countries, whether in Africa, the Middle East or Europe. Reception staff had itchy fingers.

"Why are there wreaths on all these tables?" Kurt had demanded, once, baffled.

Wreaths consisting of red and white carnations were the centrepiece on every table.

"The First Lady specifically sent these arrangements for her dinner," the events co-ordinator replied.

"Wreaths? Are you sure?"

"Yes, sir, these were the orders we received from State House."

"Let's hope this meeting will not end up a funeral," Kurt said, striding out of the banqueting room.

In Africa, top government officials never ordered a la carte as they were too afraid of being poisoned. Buffets were the only acceptable meals. One vice president went so far as to pick his cutlery from different tables and would ask for the entire crate of soft drinks to be brought to him so he could pick a bottle at random!

There was never a dull moment in the five-star world.

Celebrities had two sides: the alter ego, the side the public saw. This side was affably courteous and amiable. In a good mood, down to earth, even humble. The darker side—obnoxious, rude, unbearable, condescending and demanding—was kept for hotel staff and probably family and friends, no discounts there! The music industry had its fair share of God's gifts to mere mortals! Didn't their names leave no room for doubt? They never shied from freebies, even though with their money, they could afford the suite.

Bathroom amenities were their biggest weakness. Topping the list were pocket-sized body lotions, shampoos, conditioners and bubble bath from the Houses of Dior, Ferragamo, Nina Ricci or Armani, followed by bathrobes and towels. Bigger items ranged from picture frames to light bulbs—yes, light bulbs—bedsheets, duvets, clothes hangers, pillows, and even chandeliers. Remote controls and adaptors were taken as easily as the apples sitting in the bowl at the reception desk.

Outrageous requests ranged from monkey brains to lizards' tails and bat droppings. Caterpillars, rain-flies, sun-dried locusts and worms that had been staple diets for centuries in Africa or Asia were now the rave in Europe and America. Exotic food, and celebrities had to be the first to sample such epicurean delights. The less diva-ish requested crinkly crisps and Coca Cola. No champagne cocktails!

Crocodile killings held a fascination, as did big game hunting. One bullet shot to the brain to preserve the hide for tanning!

Tantrums and tantric beads were part of the billing. Sending a personal interior decorator and engineer to revamp a suite was par for top-notch clientele, including shipments of furniture, carpets and personal toilets. The water analysis report needed to be produced before arrival to ensure that bathing was germ-free and pure enough. Still, litres of mineral water would go down the drain.

Requests for rooms to be painted a specific colour were easy in comparison.

Prima donnas would demand for buggies to cart them to a suite or restaurant as they were unable to totter in skyscraper heels. Many wouldn't deign to speak to staff members, who were forbidden from making eye contact. The general manager was a tiny pawn on the chequered chessboard, not worthy of their time.

Suites had to be set at a certain temperature, not half a degree more or less. The lobby, public areas, toilets and ballrooms had to be partitioned off. Pressing buttons in lifts was a no-no. Middle Eastern royalty insisted on having all GSM and internet connections cut off while their convoy travelled from airport to hotel or vice versa. Afraid of a detonation via a mobile phone.

"It's so hard to have a conversation with poor people."

In relaying the encounter to Laila, Kurt mentioned how he had raised his eyebrows in surprise when escorting the influencer to the penthouse suite. She looked down her newly done nose. "Do you know what I mean? They just don't understand things the way we do."

The lift doors opened; she waved her hand in the air. "Well, you wouldn't know what I'm talking about as you're *only* working class!"

She strutted into the elegant suite, sighing loudly. The social media age had produced the biggest egos with the smallest brains!

Money talked. Though not enough. Money couldn't buy happiness, friendship, manners or love. It could buy shame, destruction, greed, sin and embarrassment. Any vice could be bought for a price.

There were, however, many wonderful personalities who went through these revolving doors. Down-to-earth celebrities and humanitarians.

Laila remembered how dignified and humble Nelson Mandela was. He'd had an aura about him that oozed charisma and gentleness. He stood patiently for every photograph requested by staff.

"Come in, please come in."

Kurt had stood hesitantly at the entrance of the presidential suite. He'd wanted to check that everything was in order, never expecting to find Mr Mandela sitting at the dining table.

"Mr Petticoat, come. I remember you escorted me up to this magnificent suite yesterday. Don't you hate eating breakfast alone? Sit down with me."

Kurt sat on the chair that was pulled out.

One of the nicest ten-minute conversations he'd had ever, he later told Laila. 'Gracious' was the word that came to mind in Mandela's presence.

Meryl Streep was delightful and ordinary. She was charming, spending several minutes signing autographs for staff and guests in the lobby. Mohammed Ali, even suffering with Parkinson's, exuded a charisma that floated like a butterfly around him. Michael Jordan was large in person, like his personality. Prince Albert of Monaco sparkled brighter than his invisible armour, reflecting humility and humour, a passionate environmentalist.

Ben Kingsley and David Attenborough were funny and kind. Brad Pitt, Gerard Butler, Tom Hanks, Matt Damon and Ben Affleck were not only gorgeous but genuine.

Men were easy-going. Women less so.

Laila knew that, living in a hotel, her family had to sacrifice their privacy. There were no secrets, absolutely nothing the staff didn't know. The fights that took place, the food they ate and the friends they made. It was a price she was willing to pay.

Are friendships more fragile in the hotel industry?

Are friendships transitory?

Are women fickle, picking and dropping friends like shopping in a supermarket? How easy is it to pick up an item and drop it carelessly into the trolley? A few aisles down, why not discard of it? It wasn't exactly what they were looking for, after all.

Laila pondered these questions.

Friendships were depicted as wonderful relationships, but surely no woman hasn't experienced the betrayal of a best friend, the sudden silence for no apparent reason, the snubbing. The lucky few whose friendships spanned many years didn't realise what blessings they had. Like a bad marriage, some friendships required a divorce.

"Shouldn't we hold on to friendship?" Laila's hazel eyes locked with Lakshmi's caramel ones.

Lakshmi had continued knitting the pale pink sweater for her fourteen-month-old granddaughter. Her daughter was passionate. She was Castor and Pollux, astrology twins. Lakshmi often said she'd got two for the price of one! Most times, Laila would answer her own questions, too impatient to wait for an answer.

Laila's fall-out with Phyliss was over the high chair she'd insisted Laila have when Lalita was born. Laila had sensed something brewing a couple of months ahead. Phyliss had become distant. Coffee and dinner arrangements were systematically cancelled. The weekly lunch was never on the right day, like Wednesdays had been permanently moved.

Phyliss had practically lived in the hotel the last three years. Laila understood that, with the birth of Phyliss' fifth child, things couldn't remain the same, but the distance Phyliss had gradually meted out between them bothered Laila. Phyliss had accused her of being a bad friend. Not being there for her.

Her daughter was five weeks old; sitting in a high chair was impossible. But Phyliss persisted. She wanted the chair back. In the last two weeks, she had called every day.

"When can I have the chair back?"

"Do you think you could drop the chair this week, Laila?"

"I know this is silly, but I need to get the chair back."

"I sound like a broken record, but I really need the high chair."

Yes, she *was* sounding like a broken record. Why didn't she understand that the chair was being reupholstered?

Finally, Phyliss had sent her chauffeur to Laila with a note.

Laila, I've waited long enough. Please give Stephen the high chair. He won't leave without it. Thanks.
Philly xxx

The note infuriated Laila—not only the diminutive, but the Judas kisses as well! Wouldn't any normal person react the same way? Ten minutes earlier, housekeeping had dropped off the chair, looking as good as new. In better condition than when given.

Laila felt like a ticking time bomb ready to detonate.

"She had given me the chair, for heaven's sake. How can she ask for it back?" Laila's eyes flashed angrily in Lakshmi's direction.

It had been considerate to have the chair reupholstered. Apparently, Phyliss, her friend of three years, thought differently.

Lakshmi shook her head in amusement. Her fiery daughter was upset. In this state, she always rambled on.

"For weeks, she's been playing a cat-and-mouse game with me. If she couldn't handle a baby in her old age, she shouldn't have had one!"

"Don't be nasty, Laila. I didn't bring you up like that," Lakshmi said, her amusement turning to annoyance.

"Because she's not being nasty?"

Phyliss was forty-two. Seeing Laila pregnant a few months ago had whetted her appetite for another child.

"I'm twenty-five, just starting a family. She already has four children. Her son is twelve."

Lili and Lalita were real-life ragdolls for Annie's three girls. They were jostled like sacks of potatoes, tugged and hauled. Carried on tiny hips, preened and plumed. Fought over as to whose turn it was to carry Lili and tiny Lalita with not a word of admonition from Phyliss.

With Phyliss's note crumpled in her fist, Laila had dragged the blue and white "Tiny Tykes" high chair over to the waiting chauffeur.

"Give this to your madam," she said curtly to him.

He refused to make eye contact. The messenger was being shot! He couldn't have looked more uncomfortable or miserable.

Phyliss' phone call came some time later. "Laila darling, thanks for the chair. You didn't tell me you were having it reupholstered."

Really? Laila thought. How many times in the last few weeks had she repeated the phrase to Phyliss? Why was she pleading ignorance? Did she think Laila had refrained from returning the high chair on purpose?

Laila's silence had spurred Phyliss on. "Have I hurt you in some way?" Laila could hear the crocodile tears on the other end of the phone line. Phyliss was cleverly shifting the blame, feigning innocence. She knew what she had done. This was the climax to her distancing tactics.

"You know what you've done, Philly darling." Two could tango. Yes, she knew that Phyliss would make mud-cakes of her reputation to their common friends, but Laila wasn't going to let her off so easily. She wouldn't swim with hippos in murky waters.

"Why the fuss, Laila? I told you from the beginning that the chair was on loan."

"On loan?" Laila asked, baffled. *When you gave me the chair, you never dreamt of getting pregnant,* she thought angrily. Had she intended to put her twelve-, ten-, nine-, and eight-year-old children in there?

"In the last few weeks, you've been so wrapped up in your own life, you've no time for me."

"Fuck you!"

"Laila!" Lakshmi shouted, disconnecting the phone. "How dare you talk like that? You need to wash your mouth out. I don't care who's to blame."

Laila thought she would explode. She didn't need to hear Phyliss lie.

"How can people like Phyliss look themselves in the mirror? She's twisted the entire situation to her advantage, and now *I* am the bad one?" Anger gurgled out of Laila, who paced the cream carpet of the fifth-floor hotel apartment.

The view from the French windows was stunning. The lush greenery of Uhuru Park in February was breathtaking. Jacaranda trees heaved with lilac flowers, the spectacular purple carpet of freshly fallen flowers on the ground as beautiful as the blossoms on the trees. Bougainvillea shrubs of every colour from red to pink to white to orange were abundant. The flame trees that lined Haile Selassie Avenue were covered with bright orange blossoms, a fiery spectacle. The verdant grass of Uhuru Park stretched the length of the highway.

The scenery was lost to Laila as tears welled in her eyes. She brushed them away with the back of her hand.

Why was she crying? Phyliss wasn't worth it. But a three-year friendship had vanished in a couple of minutes. It couldn't have meant much to Phyliss if she could turn the tables so easily and point an accusing finger at Laila. Did she think that Laila was stupid because of her age?

Laila wiped the hot tears away. She could feel her mother behind her.

"Friendships come and go, Laila. You have to learn to move on," Lakshmi said consolingly, anger at Laila's use of abusive language forgotten.

"Why?" Laila sounded like a child. "Does friendship have an expiry date? I shouldn't take it personally. The unanswered phone calls and text messages. I saw Phyliss trying to make herself as small as possible in the supermarket the other day. How low will she stoop to avoid me? Suddenly, I'm to blame. I haven't been there for her? The high chair was a pretext to end our friendship. It's not fair!"

"Life isn't fair, my child. We have to make our own happiness. Losing a friend is never easy, especially over something so silly. But it happens. Don't shed tears."

Laila was silent.

"You're young, Laila. You'll meet many people as the years go by. Remember today's lesson and never knowingly hurt anyone."

Laila gave her mother a lopsided smile.

"And I never want to hear such language again, my child. It's not befitting. No matter how angry you may get. Understood?"

***

June 2004

Laila stared at the Facebook page. She'd been debating with herself for a few days. Should she get in touch with Phyliss? Her eldest son was getting married. How many years had gone by? Eighteen? Twenty? Their last conversation had been one of anger.

How would Phyliss react to receiving a message from her out of nowhere? Laila tried to put herself in Phyliss' shoes. Finally, she made up her mind. It wouldn't hurt to send a message of congratulations.

We all get hurt at some point in life. Time, they say, is a great healer. Would it be in Phyliss' case? Learning to place a plaster on the hurt and anger had helped her to move on, and she knew she wasn't blame-free either. She had been young and feisty, her temper getting the better of her. Now, she was at the age Phyliss had been all those years ago. She had doubts, insecurities and questions that had never crossed her mind at twenty-five. She could understand Phyliss better now.

Was it the right decision? Would she get a reply from Phyliss? Or would she still hold a grudge? Time would tell.

Laila clicked the send button.

CHAPTER 5

"ROYALS"

April 1990

Changing countries never bothered Laila. She enjoyed travelling. Meeting new people and discovering new places fascinated her. It opened up her senses and made her culturally and intellectually aware of others.

She sometimes worried that Lili and Lalita would resent having to change schools every two years. Leaving friends behind to start making new friends all over again was difficult, but the girls had grown up with change, adapting well.

The first move from Kenya had been the most difficult for Laila. To leave familiarity for the unknown world of Saudi Arabia was overwhelming. But fear had been the only thing standing in her way, and she wasn't going to be afraid, though Lili was three years old and Lalita only eighteen months. She'd known parting from Lakshmi was going to be difficult. Painful.

"You have your own family. That's where you belong. There are many women who would be glad to be in your place. Look forward to the good things that are coming your way. Your husband and daughters need you, not tears." Ever stoic, Lakshmi had chided Laila.

The nomadic lifestyle began. It was fun, interesting and educational. It could also be tedious, frustrating and lonely, especially as the sparkle of the early years wore off for Laila. Making friends was harder. The fast-evolving world of technology wasn't helping; friends could be un-friended or blocked! As her daughters grew up, there were no more school mums to talk to. No coffee mornings or afternoon teas. The girls had been the ice-breaker. They were now leading their own lives in Europe. Both had been like rubber bands, bouncing back into shape with each move.

Laila, on the other hand, felt that her elasticity was wearing thin. Thirty years of moving was taking its toll. Airports and long flights were no longer exciting, but time-consuming and claustrophobic. The security checks worsened with each year that went by. Why was she always behind the person who had a water bottle in their handbag and toiletries above the limit? Why were the majority of people sporting headphones and hoodies? In the seventies, taking a flight had meant dressing up, men in suits and ties and women in their Sunday best.

What happened to conversation? It had been replaced by texting. For Laila, it was time-consuming trying to decode messages written in a lingo that had no idea of spelling or punctuation and hadn't even a passing acquaintance with grammar. What happened to being social, to interacting with others?

The generation was at ease with a smartphone or tablet but less so with each other. It was easy to be unkind on social media.

Technology was taking over the world, and not necessarily for the better. The young generation were in their element shopping online, using self-checkout or the myriad of machines, be it in a bank or at a take-away, replacing human contact. Laila thought it was sad. Impersonal.

Laila was old-fashioned. The check-out till didn't recognise a smile. Headphones were a sure sign: don't talk to me!

Social skills were fast becoming a thing of yore. Nothing seemed genuine.

She was nostalgic for the eighties and nineties.

She knew she wasn't alone in thinking this way. Cost-cutting measures in recent years had relegated top management and their families to economy travel instead of business, a luxury that was missed. Expats working with Kurt complained constantly to colleagues about privileges. Why didn't they have the same benefits as the boss? The same salary scale for all and all for the same salary scale! Everyone was on first-name terms; therefore, they thought they deserved the same advantages.

Businesses had become political camps. It was survival of the fitness and who you knew to get to the top. Gone were the days when an employee was content with a firm handshake or a pat on the back no longer existed. Good employees were overlooked when less-capable colleagues would go to any lengths to climb the ladder. One piece of silver was enough to betray colleagues. Many were only too willing to shine shoes brighter. Capability was outweighed by corruption of the mind. Like in the animal kingdom where the victor rules supreme and the loser has to leave the jungle in search of new territory, some stooped lower still, like hyenas waiting for the kill to be made. Once the groundwork was done, they would circle to feed on the carcass.

Movies depicting the good guy getting the longed-for promotion and recognition were exactly that, movies. Fantasy. In real life, the good guy is thrown out of the boss's office, the door slammed and the key thrown away. Goodbye promotion, hello miserable life. A tongue heavy with honey to suck up to the boss is the only qualification needed. More so in the five-star world! Politics were not only for governments, Laila was convinced.

***

Laila stared out of the tinted limousine window. She was in Saudi Arabia. The land of Aladdin and Jasmine. Kurt had picked her and the girls up in style in a navy BMW Series 7 with cream leather and mahogany interior.

Jeddah couldn't have been more different from Nairobi. It was clean and organised, with vertiginous glass skyscrapers and plush malls dazzling in the sweltering Arabian heat. She wasn't half an hour in the country, and already missed the ever-moving cumulus clouds and warm Kenyan sunshine. The lush greenery of rainbow bougainvillea, blood-red hibiscus bushes, fragrant frangipane and purple jacaranda trees were replaced by huge roundabouts with perfect beds of petunia, marigolds or azaleas. Lawns were perfectly manicured, water sprinklers whirring in the hazy August heat.

The colourful *kitenge* outfits of the African women bustling to the markets with sisal baskets on their heads or babies securely tied to their backs were replaced by women clothed in black abayas: slits for eyes, black socks on their feet, and black gloves to cover their hands. They looked more like characters from a sci-fi movie. Groups of these other-world creatures huddled together on shopping sprees.

Laila couldn't fathom how any woman could succumb to losing all sense of identity, dressed as a nonentity. Girls as young as six years of age were already shrouded in abayas.

Laila remembered an experience she'd had in a supermarket. A boy of not more than seven had kicked her in the shin.

"Ouch!" she'd let out a yelp.

Holding her shin, she tried to elevate the pain. He stood smugly glaring at her while his mother pretended not to have noticed what had transpired.

"*Shoo ada*! Why did you do that?" Laila asked, using the familiar Arabic term.

"Close abaya, woman."

"What? How dare you, little brat." Laila looked meaningfully at his mother, shrouded in an elaborate bejewelled abaya. The eyes behind the slits glared at Laila. If looks could kill, Laila would be shuddering on the floor in the throes of death.

"*Haram!*" the woman spat contemptuously. She spun on her heels, shepherding four children away, the son the eldest among three girls. Clearly, he was ruling the roost already.

"Sorry, ma'am, about that, but please remember to button the abaya fully," the Indian supermarket employee whispered, while pretending to stack the shelf with bottles of non-alcoholic beer.

Laila looked down to realise that her legs were bare from the knee down. Her abaya was flapping wide open.

"Thank you," she mouthed.

It was far too hot to don clothes *and* the abaya. Laila had boldly left the house in panties and bra.

Not a good idea. The law of the land deemed that women had to be swaddled in an abaya—no flesh in sight! Displaying jeans or skirts was frowned upon, God forbid shorts or a dress. Blatantly brandishing her flesh had warranted the kick!

Laila swiftly came to learn in Saudi Arabia that Arab men prize their son or sons first, then their horses and camels, cars came next, followed by daughters, and lastly wives.

The country lacked nothing, except freedom for their women. Shopping malls were towering structures of marble or granite. Prestigious. Dior, Chanel, Versace, Prada, YSL, Valentino, Cerruti, Vuitton were brand names found even in the smallest mall. Supermarkets were monstrous spaces with aisles large enough to have three trolleys pass comfortably, displaying every conceivable product. Pork and alcohol were the only exceptions, but there were many places where these two items could be found. It was a matter of knowledge and frequenting the right people. Johnnie Walker had walked kilometres in Saudi Arabia.

It was a man's world.

Supermarket tills were tended to by men, as were all boutiques or department stores. There were no fitting rooms—nudity taboo. Goods could be returned with no fuss.

Beauty and hairdressing salons were heavily curtained with no signage, a women-only realm.

Restaurants had a women-and-family section and a men-only section. Waiters not only served food and drinks but acted as messengers for couples, be they lovers or friends. Hurriedly scribbled notes would be passed from one section of the restaurant to the other. Girls or women coyly sipping mint tea were not as coy as they looked. It was fun to watch. The mobile hadn't yet made its appearance on the market—the good old days when life was simple and stalking someone was physical!

Furtive looks, accidental touching of hands and discreet passing of notes were the way the opposite sex communicated in public. Men walking hand in hand in public was a common sight. Homosexuality was rife. If you couldn't interact with the opposite sex, what other choice did you have? Everything was taboo, *haram*. Everyone wanted a bite of juicier forbidden fruit!

Women entered hotel lobbies, restaurants and malls with one pair of shoes and a handbag and left by a side or back entrance wearing another pair, toting a different handbag. The way a Pakistani or Indian driver could recognise his "madam" was by her shoes and handbag.

"Isn't that your madam? Where is she going in that Mercedes?" Laila had heard a driver say, as he leant on the sleek silver BMW. He looked questioningly in the direction of his fellow chauffeur.

"Are you crazy? I don't know that woman." In rapid Hindi, he told the newcomer in the country to shut up. "Don't ever talk about the women. You *have* no opinion or suggestion in this country. You're here to work, that's all. Do you want to lose your job and your thick head? Get your money at the end of the month and keep quiet. Understand?"

Infidelity was booming. It was a risky game, a means of meeting up with the opposite sex. The price for a woman should she be caught would certainly be death or imprisonment.

"Hey Ajay, didn't Sheikh Bin Moktar check in with a short woman yesterday afternoon?" the concierge asked the parking valet.

"Man, she must have grown a few inches last night." Ajay exchanged a knowing smile with his colleague.

Day rooms were fashionable in this part of the world, and hotels had no means of controlling rooms booked.

The pious veil was used as a way of hiding or being hidden. Who would dare ask for the veil to be lifted to check the identification given? Adolescent boys would don an abaya and veil to listen in on group conversations in shopping malls and report back to fathers and older brothers. Homosexual lovers could meet in public on a rendezvous with no one the wiser.

Not being able to drive was a welcome relief for Laila. The luxury of having a chauffeur was a dream. Struggling to find parking or idling in traffic jams was tedious. Laila didn't understand expat women who moaned about not being able to drive in Saudi Arabia. If you were born with a silver spoon, then why would you want to eat with your hands?

"Is this paradise?" Lakshmi winked cheekily.

She and Amit were visiting Laila in her new home after a year of being apart.

The grandeur and luxurious lifestyle was mind-boggling. It was hard on the eyes, the sheer monstrosity of the infrastructure. The decadent greenery of Kenya was replaced by dusty palms and sand dunes. Most villas were miniature palaces with stained glass windows, marble floors, swimming pools and private zoos with tigers, lions and cheetahs lazing around in diamond-studded collars behind high walls. High gates kept untold secrets and sadness. Bentleys, Mercedes, Rolls Royce and Lexuses sped down eight-lane highways. There were no speed limits. Jaeger-LeCoultre watches and diamond bracelets adorned wrists. In other parts of the world, the only accessory on a wrist would be a shopping bag, the supermarket's name emblazoned on both sides—Spar, Sainsbury's, Carrefour, Walmart, Shoprite!

"Why don't they stand up for themselves?" Lakshmi said, frustrated. "They have such an ostentatious lifestyle, but the women are as meek as lambs being led to the slaughter. They live in a golden cage."

"They can't, Ma. It's deeply inbred in them. From the minute they're born, they're conditioned to serve a man, be it their father, brother or husband. They never question their rights. It's normal to don an abaya and hide behind a veil with gloves and socks. If they dare question the dress code or voice an opinion, they would probably be beaten or locked away until they came around to seeing things the way their men do. The lucky few leave the country, never to return."

"But it's ridiculous. Why would any woman want that? Don't they want to better themselves? Surely, they want to go further in life? Women can do and be anything they want to!"

"I know that, Ma, because you've instilled that in me. I do the same with Lili and Lalita. These women don't know any better. What you don't know doesn't hurt. Many of them wouldn't recognise a classroom."

Lakshmi shook her head sadly, unable to comprehend such acceptance from women who could do so much more. Who deserved better.

Laila worked part-time at an institute for deaf and dumb children. One of her responsibilities was typing out doctor's reports on patients. It was heartbreaking to see babies and children so disabled, mentally and physically. The majority of cases were incest—father, brother, uncle or cousin. A disability was construed as a curse, black magic. The stigma was so great that many of the children were locked away in rooms, only to be brought out for the doctor's appointment wrapped up like mummies, accompanied by a maid or driver. They could be considered lucky to come for treatment; others were probably shackled, beaten and starved in a basement of a plush villa or palace.

Women lived in fear of fathers, brothers and husbands. Permission in the form of a letter was needed for them to travel alone. Life was ruled by the *mutaween*, religious police. A strand of hair peeking out was construed as enticing the opposite sex. A severe dressing down and sometimes even a rap over the shoulder with a baton would be punishment meted out. Pilipino and Indian women were targeted most by mutaween, because of their long, black luxuriant hair. The majority had left their families behind to earn money that would enable them to buy a piece of land back home, educate their children and even construct a house. The price they paid was high. Many were ill-treated, raped and starved.

Laila was approached countless times by Saudi women wanting to know why she had such short hair.

"Does your husband beat you?"

"Does he pull it? Is that why you cut it so short? Short hair no good on woman."

On arrival in the country, Laila had cut her thick curly hair that had fallen to her waist. It had been suffocating in the heat! She didn't want to entice the opposite sex, she often joked.

Wealth abounded in the country. On Fridays, wealthy families gave alms. It was the only day of the week the physically disabled or poor were seen, and only for a few minutes outside grand villas. The other days of the week, they were whisked off to the farthest ends of the city, their corner.

Laila remembered sitting demurely in the back seat of the blue BMW while the attendant filled the car. She was appalled when her driver drove off.

"We have to go back, Kiran. You haven't paid."

"Petrol is free, ma'am," Kiran said, laughing.

Laila felt like the queen being addressed in this way. The use of 'mama' in Kenya wasn't sophisticated. It sounded old and tired.

Jobs were held by every other nationality except for Saudis. Saudi men spent their time smoking shisha and stalking girls in malls. A typical day out would be bumping into women, brushing a breast or a bottom. Lo and behold, should a woman be brave enough to react adversely, the disappearing act would be like a good magic trick.

Once a week, there would be a cocktail party or dinner held by the foreign embassies for non-diplomats to enjoy a glass of Riesling, Bordeaux, Laurent Perrier Rose champagne, or something stronger. A suckling pig on a spit would be a bonus. The advantages of having a diplomatic courier!

Laila met Jeanne at a cocktail party. She was a gynaecologist who had worked in the country for many years. Casual conversation turned into friendship. The stories Jeanne recounted were atrocious.

"The women I see daily have sad lives, Laila." Jeanne tucked her blonde hair behind her ear.

"Sad?"

"I see six, maybe seven women daily with vaginas destroyed. Even with medical intervention, the patient is beyond help."

Laila's brown eyes stared in horror at Jeanne, uncomprehending. "What? Why?"

"Because the men are depraved. They use broken bottles or make the women have sex with animals for the heck of it. They beat their women, mistresses and maids. Some are so badly beaten that they are unrecognisable. Many come in limping or in wheelchairs."

Unbidden tears rolled down Laila's cheeks.

There were hundreds of cases of women treated for atrocious sexual traumas, including burns, lashings, bruising and sodomy. It was appalling. Such occurrences were never spoken of in the media or even among the Saudis.

Islam was great. *Allah Akbar*!

No one dared speak negatively about the Kingdom. The guillotine was sharpened every Friday for offenders.

Laila understood why Mounira, her beautician—a magician when it came to threading perfect eyebrows—was averse to giving massages.

She'd asked her, once. "Do you do massages, Mounira?"

"I used to but no more."

"Why? With your magic hands, I'm sure you would have queues of women."

Mounira wrung her long, tapered hands, looking uncomfortable. "Saudi ladies would ask me to do other things, saying that their husbands didn't satisfy them. I could have become rich. They were willing to pay me any amount of money."

"What did you do?"

"I would tell them to leave. The first time I thought the lady was crazy and that I heard wrong, but then I was getting more and more requests. It was getting out of hand! No pun intended! Every Saudi woman who entered my door would ask. I couldn't take it. The constant begging, some even cried. No massage, Saudi or not! I'm in this country for the money. What I make here in a month I would make in India in six months."

When Lakshmi visited, she sat out on the villa balcony with Laila. The marble floor felt cool on Laila's bare feet. The swaying palms and perfumed gardenia hedge in the compound below belied a system that didn't work. Money was the sole reason so many from the East flocked to the country.

It was sad. Men left their families behind and only returned after two years on ten weeks' vacation. The lucky few who were granted vacation after a year were far between.

On arrival, passports were handed over to the employer. A fine-tooth comb was taken to all cargo. Any religious material found that wasn't Islam-related was destroyed. Bibles were burned in huge metal drums daily. Companies advised potential employees not to pack video cassettes or even family albums. Any show of flesh was construed as *haram*. The final kiss in Walt Disney's *Cinderella* fell in this category. There were no churches nor temples nor synagogues in the country. Zero tolerance for other religions.

Laila wondered if God, Yahweh, Allah, Shiva, Buddha and Jehovah took turns in heaven, competing to see who carried out the best miracles or the worse destruction. Did they keep a scorecard? The winner takes it all? Whose prayers did they answer? The unemployed praying for a job or the corrupt boss asking for another ten percent? The murderer praying for a lesser sentence, or the hungry, homeless family?

Foreign women were treated worse than their own. According to Saudis, all foreign women were loose. Prostitutes. Their dress sense proved that. They could treat them however they wanted; it didn't matter.

Maids, whether they were Indian, Pakistani, Filipino, Ethiopian or another nationality, were raped regularly by their Saudi employers. Wives aware of what was going on under their own roofs chose to turn a blind eye. They were left alone, if the maid was the victim.

"Does Nana, your Eritrean maid, also have a Saudi employer?" Lakshmi looked questioningly at Laila.

"She works part-time, doing several hours a week at different residences. She buys her work permit through a company that makes her pay an exorbitant fee. Her husband works as a driver here in Jeddah, so they live together. She's lucky to work in the same city as her husband."

Lakshmi nodded, understanding how life in Saudi Arabia differed immensely to other countries. "We should count our blessings, my child."

Laila smiled her agreement.

"I like your neighbours," Lakshmi added.

A social butterfly, she had already introduced herself to the other ladies.

The twelve villas in the compound were for the hotel management employees, from the executive chef to the chief engineer. A medley of nationalities from European to Indian to American, Lebanese, Palestinian and Far Eastern.

The houses were beautiful and spacious, with three floors of white marble. The staircase itself belonged at Buckingham Palace or the Chateau of Chambord. Three large en-suite rooms with gold-plated taps in the bathrooms and separate walk-in showers. Each room had a large balcony and a fully equipped kitchen with oak cabinets any woman would die for.

"I would have gone crazy in the first few weeks if it wasn't for Divya," Laila told Lakshmi. "She welcomed me to Jeddah like a long lost relative."

Her South Indian hospitality had warmed Laila's heart, stopping the homesick tears. Her door was always open. Lili and Lalita were like sisters to her ten- and twelve-year-old daughters.

Eileen was the only white woman in the compound. Perhaps she felt like a fish out of water in the company of the other women. She refused to mingle, openly snubbing even a greeting, stating they were not of her level. There wasn't a caste system in the compound, Laila wanted to point out, but thought better.

"Eileen is a snob," Laila told Lakshmi. "She's constantly moaning about the country, the people and the weather. Why did she leave her own country if it was so perfect? She's probably left a box of an apartment in a council estate to live up the life here!

If she stopped moaning for a while, perhaps she would enjoy her time better."

Laila rolled her eyes, hardly believing that Eileen could ever enjoy life. Expatriate life meant putting up with all sorts, like drinking out of a bottle when you're not offered a glass.

Laila wondered whether she should feel privileged that Eileen deigned to speak to her, as wife of the general manager. The advantages of a title! The first time she'd come knocking on Laila's door after her arrival from England had been hilarious.

"Where is your madam?" Eileen pronounced each word carefully, raising her voice. Did the English think that shouting would make them better understood? The other person wasn't hard of hearing!

"Madam? What madam?" Laila shouted back, looking blankly at the redhead standing on her doorstep. She had hips that didn't lie; shame about the personality.

She rolled her eyes. "Do you understand English? Where. Is. The. Madam. Of. The. House?"

Laila kept a straight face. Eileen had taken for granted that Kurt would be married to a fellow countrywoman! Why not carry on the charade for a while longer?

"No madam here." Laila bobbed her head from side to side.

"You people are so stupid. Like it's not enough to deal with the Arabs. Do you not understand English?" Eileen's freckles turned redder with her mounting irritation.

Even if Laila had been the maid— a maid with a string of pearls and gold bangles jingling on her wrists—there was no need to be condescending.

"Imbecile!" Eileen turned in a huff to leave. She let out a loud, audible sigh.

"I'm Laila. Laila Petticoat. Kurt's wife. Is it me you're looking for?" Laila felt like Lionel Richie. She had to choke down the laughter that had welled up.

The shock on Eileen's face as she realised her gaffe was priceless.

"I'm so, *so* sorry." Her face had turned the same colour as her flaming hair. At least she had the decency to be embarrassed. "I assumed that you were British."

"Assume, making an ass of you and me!" Laila couldn't help herself from making the jibe.

Eileen was on the verge of saying something but thought better of it.

"Would you like to come in?" Laila asked sweetly.

She rued that invitation.

From then on, there was no getting rid of Eileen or her brood. She was on Laila's doorstep every day from the minute her two children left for school at 7:30 a.m. till they got back at 2:00 p.m.

"We have come to play with Lili," Yonah, Eileen's daughter, stated.

The girls hadn't been home for more than fifteen minutes, and already Yonah and Ronan were breaking down the door.

They were the same age as Lili and Lalita. The difference was that they were badly brought up. No please or sorry. Thank you was used sparingly, and either said feebly or not at all. No may I or can I, no manners full stop! They opened cupboards, helping themselves to cookies, crisps or dried fruit. The fridge that was off-limits to Lili and Lalita was raided daily for juice packs or chocolate.

Eileen insisted they were vegetarian, but that didn't stop them from eating chicken nuggets or fish fingers. In Eileen's house, food consisted of cheese and egg sandwiches seven days a week. Sliced carrot, courgettes, celery stalks and fruit were considered treats.

Familiarity breeds contempt, and Eileen was a constant fixture. Part of the furniture! Another Urvashi in her life.

"Are you going to Heera Shopping Centre today? Can you buy me a few things, Laila? It's far too hot for me."

Isn't it too hot for me? Laila thought.

The few things were milk, bread, cheese, yoghurt, ice cream, biscuits and toilet paper! When had she become Eileen's personal maid? There was rarely a refund for items purchased, and Laila felt embarrassed having to ask.

Her kindness was being taken advantage of. *No* and *sorry* must have been the hardest words in the English language. And thank you. Why say thank you? It's so demeaning!

The daily visits from Yonah and Ronan added to her growing rancour. Once they'd left the girls' bedroom, it resembled one of Etna's eruptions. Toys strewn across the floor, under the beds, in the cupboards, on the bookshelves.

"The girls have to arrange their toys after they finish playing," Laila hinted.

"They're kids, for heaven's sake." Eileen brushed it off. "I don't force my children to do anything they don't want to. Housekeeping can do that when they come on Sundays and Wednesdays."

That's why they're impolite and obnoxious. Do you have housekeeping in England? Laila wondered.

A few days later, Lakshmi opened the door to Yonah and Ronan while Laila was busy in the kitchen. It wasn't long before the sound of yelling brought her rushing to the sitting room. The once prestigious white-and-gold sofa had been reupholstered in pink, green and yellow fluorescent marker stripes and waves. Red crayon had been smashed and crushed into the fabric and looked like bloodstains. The hand-embroidered cushion covers were also re-designed. The settee looked like something out of *The Little Shop of Horrors*!

"Who did this?" Laila glared at her daughters. They knew they weren't allowed on the sofas. They had their own sitting area under the staircase, furnished from Ikea.

Yonah stared at Laila with wide blue eyes then promptly burst into tears and dashed out of the house. Ronan sat on his heels, looking dolefully through his spectacles, sniffling as always, then sprinted out of the villa.

"They came with their box of colours," Lalita volunteered. "Ronan started drawing, then Yonah copied him."

Laila turned at the sound of an angry rap on the already ajar door. Eileen stood there, fury written all over her face. She had never bothered to knock in the past!

"What did you say to my children? Yonah can barely speak; you've traumatised her."

"Traumatised her? I didn't even speak to her." Laila pointed to the sofa, equally furious.

"Is this what you're making a big deal about? It can be easily washed off. You're unbelievable!"

"A big deal? I'm unbelievable? These are highlighter markers, and the crayon is embedded

119

in the fabric. How will it wash off?" Laila could barely control her temper.

Lakshmi touched her shoulder fleetingly.

Eileen's fury had been replaced by boredom and disinterest. "It's not like these are your sofas. Stop making such a fuss."

"Just because these sofas are not mine doesn't mean that your unruly children have the right to ruin them."

"I don't need to take this crap over something so small." Eileen grabbed Ronan, who was clutching at her skirt, and stormed off, slamming the door.

"Did you see that? How is she bringing up those kids? To destroy what doesn't belong to them? What kind of mentality is this? Can you imagine the state of her villa, if this is her attitude?" Laila fired questions in Lakshmi's direction.

"My child, calm down. Do you think she's going to lose sleep over you or your sofa? It's no skin off her back, so it makes no difference. How can she value things when she didn't earn them through hard work?"

Laila had the sofa dry-cleaned professionally, but the stains wouldn't budge. She resorted to covering them with a throw. Eileen never spoke to her again, not even a nod in her direction. This was one friendship Laila wasn't going to try to keep.

***

Weddings in Saudi Arabia were longed-for affairs. An occasion where women had free will.

Abayas were nowhere in sight, except to enter or leave the hotel ballroom. Waitresses were employed for these special events. Flowers cost a small fortune, flown in from Amsterdam. The buffets were sumptuous with whole goats or lambs slowly roasted for hours on hot coals. Fruit carvers were brought in from the Far East for these banquets. Every conceivable food could be found on heaving tables.

Laila was dumbstruck as she sat with Lakshmi. They looked like poor relatives from another planet in their long dresses. The owner of the Porsche showroom was marrying off one of his daughters, and Kurt had received an invitation for his wife plus one.

The gowns were worthy of a night at the Oscars. In any other country, the jewellery worn would have needed heavy security, but there wasn't a guard in sight.

"Are those diamonds and emeralds real?" Lakshmi whispered.

"You bet. There's nothing fake on these ladies."

Necks were straining with cut diamonds, rubies, sapphires and emeralds. Earlobes and wrists sparkled with shimmering stones and pearls. Fingers were heavy with rings; it was a surprise the ladies could lift the glasses of juice to their lips! The Houses of Cartier, Boucheron, Fred, Van Cleef and Arpels, De Beers, de Grisogono, Bvlgari, and Tiffany & Co, to name just a few, were doing booming business in Saudi Arabia.

"None of this jewellery is on loan. Can you imagine owning what they're wearing? Mind-boggling, isn't it?" Laila said.

Lakshmi sat staring, nudging Laila ever so often to look at a diamond-studded handbag or hair accessory. They were sat with other expatriate ladies, who were as enthralled by the wealth as they were. It was like being stuck in a dream, full of dazzling light bouncing off exquisite jewels.

The air hung with the heady smell of expensive perfumes. Women were heavily made-up, and hairstyles were elaborate, whether dyed ebony or golden blondes. The bride made a breathtaking entrance. She was a vision in a fairy-tale white gown. Hand-sewn crystals and pearls made up the bodice. Her tiara weighed a few kilos.

In the gardens of the hotel, her father had lined up twelve Porsches in every colour for her to pick from. It seemed a little pointless to Laila. It wasn't as if the bride would be driving anywhere, as a Saudi woman in the nineties. The bride settled on an amethyst-coloured car. The groom would be celebrating with his friends in a privately owned villa, with several belly dancers and leggy Russian women. Cristal Roederer champagne, several bottles of fine whisky, cognac and Monte Cristo cigars. A night of debauchery.

The evening continued with a Lebanese singer and an all-women Filipino band. It was a scene from another world. The women were having the time of their lives, dancing, clapping and ululating. It was incredible. The gift bag at the end of the evening consisted of Chanel products—No.5 perfume, lipstick *and* a purse!

It was ironic how one part of the world could live in the lap of luxury while the other part didn't have clean drinking water or sanitation.

Two years rolled by in a blink of an eye. For all its shrouded secrecy, Laila enjoyed her time and experiences in this Middle Eastern part of the world. People were always aghast when she said she'd spent two years in Saudi Arabia.

"How could you have lived there?"

"As a matter of fact," she'd tell them. "We lived rather well."

CHAPTER 6

"IMAGINE"

June 1992

The salvo of AK-47s broke the silence. The sound was distant but audible. Dawn was breaking over the horizon.

Laila prised her eyes open. How long had she been sleeping? She was exhausted. If only she could sleep for a hundred years like Sleeping Beauty. Every bone in her body ached. She was lying on the thin mattress, the threadbare blanket tightly wrapped around her.

The sky was suffused with iridescent hues of pink. The flaming orange sun peeked out majestically from her night of rest, ready to tackle the day with scorching rays of heat, which by midday would turn the hazy light into a mirage, outlining profiles in shadowy waves. The beauty of nature was overshadowed by fear and death. Of hate and grief.

The fire of the night before had died out, leaving a smoky odour. The ashes, a dull grey, rose with the slight wind, creating tiny confetti that fell on her. Laila brushed the flakes off her face and rubbed her dry, cracked lips. She pulled at the skin with her lower teeth, drawing blood. She winced, stopping immediately.

When was the last time she'd had a shower? She could smell the acrid sweat on her unwashed body and feel the thick heaviness of her tongue. Her mouth felt furry, like a dentist had numbed her gums. Colgate would be like caviar in her mouth. Her jeans were stiff with layers of caked mud and blood and God only knew what else. Laila could no longer differentiate the putrid smell of decomposing flesh from her bodily odour. It was overwhelming and all-encompassing. There was no getting away from it. Her obsessiveness with cleanliness had no place in this horrific environment. Her two showers a day had been reduced to no shower in days.

When she'd volunteered to work at the border, she never imagined what it would entail.

The war between the Tutsis and Hutus raged uncontrollably.

The pitiful few who managed to escape to the border of Brazzaville were worn and broken people. They trudged the dusty roads with vacant eyes. The same dusty roads a few months ago had been plied by women in colourful kitenges balancing woven baskets or colourful plastic buckets on their heads, singing while they marched to the market with their wares, mostly piping hot delicacies: corn cakes or deep-fried plantain. Baskets of oranges, papayas and bananas. Avocado and aubergine pyramids had tottered on heads. Money pouches whipped out of cleavages to complete the sale of fresh, local fare.

Men wove their bicycles among the womenfolk, teasing or whistling in tune to their songs. Young girls huddled in clusters on the kerb waiting for their turn at the open-air hairdressing salon. The deft fingers of the hairdresser would weave their hair into elaborate braids.

"Sit still, girl," the hairdresser would admonish, wobbling on a wooden stool.

"The braids are too tight. It hurts."

"Looking good hurts. Tomorrow, when Pablo winks at you and compliments how pretty your hair looks, you won't remember the pain!"

Music blared from radios. Everyone was either singing or dancing or both. Children grew up with rhythm from birth, swaddled on their mother's backs. Music was in their blood. It surged through their veins, making feet light and heads dizzy with the African beat.

There was happiness. Laughter. Contentment with the little they had—and many times with practically nothing.

Now the only sound to be heard was that of gunfire, a sound many had become immune to.

Laughter was replaced by weeping or the distant howling of mangy stray dogs. Humans and animals alike were mourning the atrocities that were taking place. There was no singing nor dancing, no laughter, no men on bicycles, and no aroma of fried delicacies. The makeshift hairdressing salons were empty. The wooden stool lay broken in the nearby ditch. No tottering baskets of fruits or vegetables. The women now just scuttled away at the slightest sound. Fear was everywhere. It lingered in the air, outside mud huts and pavements.

Those once happy days seemed like a figment of the imagination. Eyes that looked back were dead and lifeless. They could have been corpses. Women stared vacantly, lost in another world.

A rifle butt at the back of a temple couldn't elicit a reaction.

They were too broken by months of fighting. There was desperation and desolation. The Hutus were 'weeding out the cockroaches'. The cockroaches being the Tutsi, who the Hutus considered superior. Human stupidity, as Einstein said, was infinite!

How could humans be so utterly cruel to each other? It was beyond comprehension.

Kurt had tried to dissuade Laila from volunteering, but she had been adamant. How could she watch such atrocities and not even try to help? The turning point had come when Timothee the Belgian chef returned gaunt and broken from a visit to his wife and children. After months, resident permits had been granted for his family, who were from Rwanda, to join him in the Democratic Republic of Congo.

The optimistic, strong, muscular man who had left to bring his family home returned alone. After some time, Timothee confided in Laila. "I remember what the enraged Hutu shouted, as he aimed a rifle at my wife, shooting her just below the heart. 'You, *Mzungu*! Why did you marry a Tutsi? Don't you know you're reproducing vermin?'

"He made my daughters and I watch until she bled to death. The keening of my daughters while they watched their mother die will stay with me for the rest of my days.

"'Mama! Mama!' the little girls whispered as the tears rolled down their smooth golden cheeks.

"The Hutu then grabbed both girls out of my grasp and shot them between the eyes. The six- and eight-year-old girls flopped to the dusty road, lifeless.

"I let out a howl as I made a dash to where my family lay. I clutched the three of them to my chest.

"'Move, *Mzungu*,' one of the men said, and kicked me in the ribs. It hurt. It didn't hurt as much as the pain in my heart. 'Get out of the road,' he told me.

"'Please shoot me. I can't live without my family. Please,' I begged.

"The four military men roared with laughter. Enjoying their victim's grief. 'No, we will not kill you.' The leader of the pack was tall. His face was as black as thunder. 'Take your passport and leave.'

"He beckoned to his cohort, who dragged my limp body into the vehicle. With the little energy left in me, I struggled to stay by my family. My passport was tossed at my feet as I curled in the foetal position at the back of the truck.

"I pleaded with them to let me bury my family. 'Please,' I whimpered. 'Please.'

"To which one of them replied, 'Cockroaches don't need to be buried. Let them rot there.'

"The leader's features were contorted in anger and disdain. 'Move. You're wasting my time, *Mzungu*,' he bellowed. He shoved me out of his way.

"I willed them to kill me as they drove on the bumpy road. To spare me the life I would have with the image of his dying wife and daughters. The two Hutus ignored me as the music blared from the car radio. It had been so easy to pull the trigger."

The look in Timothee's eyes when Laila held his cold hand was haunted and lost—dead, like his family. Every drop of blood had been wrung from his heart.

"They wouldn't let me bury them. I had to leave them by the roadside, to be dumped in a mass grave. Why, Laila? What did they do to deserve this?"

Laila had no words.

"They escorted me to the airport, waiting until I boarded the flight. I was allowed the bloodstained clothes on my back and my passport. They thought they had done me a favour by sparing my life. How could they think that?"

Laila's decision to lend a helping hand had led to over four weeks living in conditions far removed from the five-star world she was used to.

Lili and Lalita had been left in the loving hands of Madeleine, the Congolese maid who adored them. The girls were just a little older than Timothee's daughters.

It had been heart-wrenching, seeing his raw pain when they passed him in the restaurant. He was a tormented man. Inconsolable. Grief was etched in every line on his face, flowing through every vein in his body. He worked relentlessly day and night. Kurt tried to persuade him to take some days off, but he staunchly refused.

The camps where Laila volunteered were overflowing with a desperate need for clean water, food, and basic sanitation. Laila met Narmin and Julia, also volunteers, who had lived in the Democratic Republic of the Congo for years. It was home for them. They spoke Lingala like the locals. Laila only had admiration for them; this was friendship at first sight. The three of them shared a bond. They cried together when things got too much and smiled at the sparse joy they found in the starry night sky or a child's spontaneous laughter at being tickled. A toffee or sweet was manna from heaven, eliciting broad smiles and a few minutes of respite from the eerie silence of the adult world.

They would hold the hands of victims and shed tears, though the tears couldn't wash away the horrors that had been endured. They missed their families sorely, but every 'thank you' they received made up in a small way for the loneliness and sorrow.

Death hung in the air like a curtain that wouldn't close.

The woman with the sack in her hand was standing again this morning at the edge of the volunteers' camp. Today was the third day.

Laila had told her to wait yesterday while she'd bandaged a nasty gash from the butt of a rifle rammed into the leg of the ten-year-old boy.

"Does it hurt, Etienne?" Laila had asked, trying to be as gently as possible.

Etienne had tried to be brave. He hadn't winced, and even managed a weak smile when Laila was done.

With the distribution of food and water, Laila had completely forgotten about the woman. Hours whizzed by with all that needed to be done during the day.

Now she was back. She walked with a stoop, the sack weighing her down. What did she have in there? Laila wondered. In all the chaos, it was a wonder she was holding on to belongings. When the gunfire started, people usually made for safety as rapidly as they could. Life was more precious.

The woman stood silently in the distance, waiting for Laila. Laila beckoned her over wiping the trickle of sweat running down her neck with her torn T-shirt.

"Mama, what is it?" Weariness dragged at Laila's soul.

Tears filled the woman's eyes, breaking Laila's heart. She should have adjusted to the desolation and despair, but every dawn made the pain and suffering more poignant. More desperate. Laila touched her hand fleetingly, and tugged her gently into sitting on the empty rice sacks that were used as mats on the cracked and broken floor.

"What's your name?"

"Muna." She sat down, but possessively held the sack close to her.

"What do you have here, Muna?" Laila asked kindly.

She took a while before she answered. Tears ran down her cheeks, but she didn't wipe them away. "My son," she said finally.

Laila's breath caught. Had she heard right?

"They killed my son. I couldn't reach him in time. I had gone to queue for food, not long. I came back to find him dead. They slashed him with a machete." Tears fell faster, but Muna continued with her story. "I cannot let him be buried with all the others. Not piled up. Please, Mama, help me bury him. A grave, just a small grave. He is only five years old. Why would they kill such a small boy? He didn't do anything to them. He hurt no one."

Laila swallowed. *Why?* She wanted to scream her frustration and despair. The desperation she had seen in Timothee's eyes was once again reflected back at her. What was wrong with the world?

"I named him Saba. The people in my village told me seven was a lucky number in Swahili. I waited seven years before I conceived. It wasn't lucky for us. It was better if I never gave birth. How will I live without him?"

She opened the sack slowly.

Saba looked like he was asleep. He was a beautiful child with a thick curly afro and smooth skin. He was thin but healthy. While he lived, Muna had fed him the choicest morsels. His mother had meticulously washed him.

Whatever trauma he had suffered at the hands of his attackers had been disguised with clean clothes and a pair of mismatched shoes on tiny feet. Muna had embalmed his body with herbs from the forests to keep decomposition at bay, but they couldn't last much longer. Already there was a faint smell.

How could Laila help this grieving mother? Where could the child be buried in the sea of tents? Muna looked at Laila with woebegone eyes. Pleading.

"Where do you come from, Muna?"

"A village fifty kilometres from here, Mama."

Muna was a striking woman with high cheekbones and full lips. There wasn't a blemish on her dark skin. Her eyes were black like coal, flecked with gold. The blue and white kitenge around her waist, dirty and torn, depicted the Virgin Mary with a rosary around her hands. Her headscarf was of the same material. She had on two or three T-shirts, all tattered in many places. Her slippers were tattered and held together by string entwined to keep them in place. The soles of her feet were sore with small blisters, deep cracks and callouses.

Laila went to the makeshift shelter she shared with Narmin and Julia. She removed the tired twenty-dollar bill from her knapsack pocket. It was the last note she had. It wasn't much but would get Muna back home to bury Saba on the family land.

"It's not much, Muna." Laila handed the bill to Muna and held her hand for a while.

Sorry wouldn't bring her son back. It wouldn't stop the fighting raging between two tribes. It wouldn't lessen or numb the physical and mental pain that so many were living through.

Was it so hard to live in harmony? To love one's neighbours?

"Thank you, Mama. God will repay your kindness. Saba can rest in peace. Thank you."

She picked up the sack and walked slowly among the crowds of people, lost, grieving, hurt, desperate, lonely, anguished and weary.

What words could be used to elevate their pain and suffering? When would it stop? Would they find peace?

At the end of the long day, the small fire took time to flare into a flame. Wood was scarce. Laila sat huddled with a few of the usual people who met at this time of dusk. It was cold. The rains would start soon. A lone owl hooted in the moringa tree. A doleful sound, an echo of the woe they felt. The group would usually talk about their days, but mostly sat in silence. The distant gunfire ceased. Even enemies needed respite. The silence would be broken from time to time by a gut-wrenching howling. The pain was too much to be kept inside. Insanity taking over.

"A lady called Muna came to see me today," Laila said eventually. "Her story was sad. I know all the stories here are sad, but this was more poignant."

"I know Muna," Narmin said. "She used to sell delicious cakes made from local flour. She never lets her son out of her sight. He's her pride and joy. She lost her husband to malaria a couple of years after her son was born."

"They call her Diana, like the princess, because of her shy smile. That's her Christian name," Martha contributed. She was Tutsi and a shoulder to cry on no matter what ethnicity. "I like her."

"Her son was massacred. She's been walking around with his body wrapped in a sack for a few days. She didn't want him buried in a mass grave. I gave her a few dollars to get her home so that she can bury him on the family land."

No one spoke. There was nothing to say.

Whether Muna would manage to get home to bury her precious child was the thought on everyone's mind, but no one dared voice it out loud. It would be bad luck.

Suddenly, Laila missed her family unbearably. She needed to see Lili, Lalita and Kurt. She had to get away. Four weeks felt like four years. The constant fear and wretchedness was too much to bear.

"I can't stay. It's far too much for me." Laila put her head in her hands. Even tears wouldn't come. A shawl of hopelessness was wrapped tightly around her shoulders, making her shiver uncontrollably.

"The Red Cross van leaves tomorrow at five-thirty a.m.," Julia said softly. "Luca is in charge. You're in good hands with him." She put an arm around Laila's shoulders trying to stem the shaking and squeezed Laila's hand. "Hang in there," she whispered.

The next morning, Laila clutched her knapsack, which held several dirty clothes and a pair of tennis shoes that were no longer white. She hugged Narmin and Julia. They were silently crying. They had gone through hell together, but their hell wasn't as scorching and fiery as what the Tutsi and Hutu were battling with. The end was in sight for Laila, but the war still raged.

***

The road back to Kinshasa was horror after horror. She had been at the centre of the violence, but her mind and hands had been kept busy tending to the needs of others. Looking out at it through the window of the van made it harsher. Laila couldn't imagine how much worse it was in Rwanda.

People wandered broken and beaten. Many were already dead, even though they put one foot in front of the other. Women with sightless eyes. How many times were they gang-raped in front of husbands and children? How many of their children, husbands, brothers and fathers were killed? Pregnant women had babies slashed from their wombs and killed before their eyes. The bloodcurdling screams couldn't erase the horrors they had seen. Did they know where they were walking to?

Bodies piled one on top of the other in deep pits. Some alive, but gravely wounded, struggled to climb free. If lucky, they would be helped out. Otherwise, they would lie in the decomposing pile until they became one of the dead, death a welcome relief.

Boys, some as young as five years of age, were rounded up in villages to be recruited by the rebels. Witchcraft promised them immunity from bullets in the form of a protection necklace, and they were initiated with a brand on the back of their necks. The younger they were, the stronger their allegiance. It was heartbreaking to see boys so young wielding a rifle. There were countless occasions when they would fall asleep with a loaded rifle and wake up having shot themselves in the foot.

In Saudi Arabia they had been driving sleek cars; here they were trained how to kill. There was no under-estimating them. They were drunk on power, and an AK-47 was deadly in their small hands. Hands that had never held a pencil but were steady as steel when aiming and firing.

The UN van had stopped at a checkpoint, where the queue was long. Laila stared out of the window in dismay.

"Look how powerful I am," the little boy said. He was shirtless. His blue shorts were torn and dirty. The back pocket hung limply from the few stitches that held it in place. His face was grubby with dried mucus. Taking aim, he shot the two mongrels that were sniffing for food in the rubbish heap.

An older boy of eleven or twelve shoved him roughly. "I'll show you how to do it properly," he gloated. Two glinting knives hung from the belt around his waist. His camouflage shirt was unbuttoned, exposing several scars.

Two successive shots rang loudly. The howl was blood-curdling as an old man hit the ground with a thud. He clutched hopelessly at each knee. Blood trickled through his knobbly fingers.

"Shoot me, please, I can't bear the pain," he pleaded, his wizened old face contorted.

"Watch, Dudu, and learn. It's not dogs you kill." He grabbed the knife from his waist and walked purposely toward the old man. He stepped savagely on his bloody right knee, and with one stroke, he severed his jugular.

The old man shuddered, taking his last breath. The few people on the road swiftly disappeared. No one wanted to be the next victim.

Incentives of land or money were enough to make these children pull the trigger. Many like Dudu and his companion didn't even need that. They were capable of killing their mother and father, sister or brother for pride of place with the rebels.

Would they ever be able to lead normal, hate-free lives?

Power, like a drug, is addictive. They learnt anger, hatred, resentment and revenge.

The van drove in the early morning sunlight. Laila noticed more and more bodies but this time of albinos lying apart from the other corpses.

"Why are there so many albinos, Luca?" It seemed odd. Piles of pink flesh with yellow hair sprawled by the roadside. Laila felt she had walked through cobwebs. The feeling was eerie. On reflex, she wiped her face.

"The witch doctors have advised AIDS patients that if they kill an albino, the virus will disappear. AIDS victims are on the rampage, and they're using this war to fight their own war with the disease. They kill them in the night and think in the morning they will be rid of their illness."

"What? And they believe them?" Laila was aghast. "How can they believe such rubbish?" She shuddered.

"When you're close to death, I think you believe in anything just to gain a few more months or years. Even days are enough."

Laila sat quietly for a long while. It wasn't enough that there was a civil war raging. Sacrificing another human being as a remedy—surely no one could be that devoid of hope as to stoop to murder?

The country believed strongly in witchcraft, and witchdoctors were glorified, respected and feared. What came out of their mouths was the bible's truth! Even when their remedies didn't work, the faithful kept on believing. Land, property and meagre savings were willingly handed over in anticipation of wealth, marriage, potency, pregnancy and cures for terminal illness. Witch doctors in this part of Africa were rich men and women.

The people were Christians in their hearts and attended church services and observed all feast days without exception. But belief in the occult was the belief in their heads. Priests were revered, but a priest could not offer a cure to a disease or pregnancy to a barren woman. All they could offer were prayers. Often, these prayers went unanswered.

The myriad people trying to get as far as possible from the horrific genocide trekked the dusty roads in sweltering heat. Women, children, men, young, old, many maimed, holding on to small possessions but no hope. A familiar face in the sea would elicit joy and untold happiness. To be reunited with a loved one was priceless.

Army trucks sped down the roads, leaving a trail of fine red dust. Military men laughed boisterously at the fear on desperate faces. A round of gunfire shot into the air made sure the civilians knew who was in charge. Laila started at the unexpected sound. She should have been used to it by now, but no matter how many times she heard it, there was no immunity to gunfire. Women let out cries of fear, taking cover.

When had the world lost its senses? When had it become unkind?

When Laila entered the apartment, Lili and Lalita stood back timidly, scared to approach. Their elegant mother had been replaced by a dishevelled woman whose hair was dirty and tangled. Mud caked her fingernails, and her face was red and patchy. She smelt.

Laila longed to hug them, but Kurt steered her toward the bedroom. His eyes shone with love.

"I've missed you, Laila."

She burst into tears and, for long minutes, clung to the man she loved deeply. Finally, she drew away. Kurt looked ridiculous in his spotless suit and impeccable white shirt and blue-striped tie. It seemed like ages since she had seen a well-dressed person.

"I think I desperately need a shower."

"You think?" Kurt tried to make light. He wiped Laila's tears. "The girls will recognise you better."

The piping hot water ran black for several minutes, washing away the dirt and grime of the last few weeks.

Laila noticed bruises that she hadn't realised she had. Black and blue angry marks on her arms and legs. She had probably got them hauling sacks of rice and flour, or the badly wounded, from one tent to another. Being slight, she'd never imagined that she had such physical strength.

Laila scrubbed herself with the loofah, but no amount of scrubbing could wash away the sadness and despair that she felt. Nor would it take away the horrors that she had seen.

She slipped back into her world. The five-star world with hot running water, room service and housekeeping. She was safe. She was loved.

What about those who weren't as fortunate? Would they have a bodyguard to protect them? Four strong walls? Where did they turn? Whose arms would they run to? How would they start over? Who loved them? Who healed them? Who helped them?

While her daughters slept, Laila sat on the edge of the bed and watched them. How peaceful they looked. They were oblivious to the horrors and hate in the world. How long could she shelter them from the atrocities spreading to all corners of every continent? She would remind them to be kind, generous, and loving. To be ready to pull others up when down, no matter what racial background or religion.

She couldn't keep them safe once they left the nest.

To be happy was all that mattered.

In the last few weeks, Laila had come to know a side of herself she'd never known she had. She was capable of huge amounts of compassion, sympathy and love. She was stronger than she imagined herself to be. She had seen sights that would haunt her, but she wouldn't let them break her. She had seen how low humans could sink, but she had also seen how high many could rise. For the few who held hatred in their hearts, there were many more who loved.

It gave her hope. The world needed hope.

CHAPTER 7

"TO MAKE YOU FEEL MY LOVE"

August 1996

"Can't believe I'm losing you," Alison Krauss sang, oblivious to how the words were affecting Laila.

Laila swallowed the lump in her throat. She wouldn't give in to tears. She pressed the temples of her head, trying to ease the niggling headache. She had to be strong, not only for herself but for her daughters.

Standing abruptly from the paisley ottoman, Laila stared out the window. The air conditioning rattled tediously.

She couldn't shake the nagging suspicion that Kurt was cheating on her. Her wonderful, kind, considerate, gallant Kurt. While other women had been running out to buy the book *Men Are from Mars, Women Are from Venus*, she had wondered why. When Steve Wright hosted Sunday Love Songs, she always thought no one could be more in love than Kurt and her. They had the greatest love story. Their marriage was solid as a rock. They were two bodies but shared one heart.

Her husband was the ideal man. He helped her with housework, especially ironing, which she

141

detested. Cooked delicious three-course meals every weekend, bought her flowers for no special reason, surprised her with the odd trinket she admired when they went shopping. He massaged her feet and painted her toenails without any prompting. He complimented her looks, her cuisine, her dress sense and even her sense of humour!

He found time to play with Lili and Lalita. He'd not only taught them to ride a bicycle and rollerblade but patiently explained fractions, multiplication and division. He was generous, had a great sense of humour, and was not only her best friend but the perfect lover. They never had to ask what the other was thinking. They didn't need to; they were finely tuned to each other's wavelength. It was uncanny how they knew each other's thoughts. Even in a crowded room, Laila knew when Kurt's eyes were on her.

She'd never thought her Kurt could be like many of the hoteliers she had met through the years, men who didn't think twice of cheating on their wives. Men who had not only one but several mistresses. They had the master key; that meant they had free range of vacant rooms and suites.

Was she to become a wife who turned a blind eye to her husband's extra-curricular activities? Would the ladies be nudging each other when she entered a room, pity in their eyes?

Laila shivered. The thought was unimaginable. They went together like the song from Grease— *rama-lama-lama-ka-dinga-da-dinga-dong*. They were the perfect couple.

They never belittled each other in public with comments like:

"You're sleeping in the doghouse tonight, darling."

"At least I won't be sleeping with a bitch tonight," mumbled under the breath.

"What do *you* know on the topic?"

"Shut up. No one wants your opinion."

"My friend, don't ever give your wife the car keys if you want your car in one piece," said with gleeful laughter.

"Don't give him the liquor cabinet keys; you'll never get them back," said with equal glee.

"I think you've had enough for one night, darling."

"Don't mind him; he's a blithering idiot!"

"It's your turn to take out the garbage, honey."

"You're garbage, take yourself out, *honey!*"

"He didn't wish me happy Mother's Day."

"Are you my mother?"

"On his salary, there's not much we can do."

"I married her for her looks, not her wit!"

"She has these little shit-chats with her friends. Chit-chats is what they call them, to make them feel better!"

Sarcasm, even rudeness, followed by the eye roll to lighten the atmosphere. Who was more in control? Who was smarter? Who was more successful? Who earned more? Laila often wondered what these couples got out of it. Satisfaction? Why were they in permanent pole position for a fight? Was it a marriage contract they had signed or a competition entry? Where was the finish line?

They were equals, Laila and Kurt. Their love raised them up, like love should. They never needed to lower nor demean each other.

The radio in the background was tuned in to 88.91 FM, BBC Radio 2. From 6:00 a.m. to 6:00 p.m., Vanessa Feltz, Chris Evans, Ken Bruce, Jeremy

Vine, Steve Wright and finally Simon Mayo kept Laila company. Their familiar voices travelled with her from continent to continent, entertaining or informing by the swimming pool, while taking a bath or behind the chopping board.

Tony Blackman's bad jokes made Laila grin—she looked forward to his Saturday morning show—and during the weekend, Graham Norton's remarks raised Laila's eyebrows. How did he get away with such comments? She aspired to be like him in public. A touch of rudeness in a jocular manner. Would she be able to pull it off without more antagonistic daggers thrown at her? Would her comments pin her to a dartboard?

Laila felt she knew the presenters personally; they were her friends. Today, even Ken Bruce couldn't bring a smile to her lips.

The changes with Kurt had been subtle. He didn't have time. He was working late. Invitations from friends were never on convenient days. Lili and Lalita were over-demanding. Why couldn't she spend more time with them? Their maths homework wasn't that difficult. The list of excuses was hollow to her ears and endless.

What had happened to her Kurt?

Lately, he never let his mobile out of his sight. He was constantly checking it. She would hear it beep at odd hours of the night and during the weekend. Naively, she'd put it down to tedious hotel messages from employees or guests. Even at his busiest, he made time for them. Maybe the hotel was running at a hundred percent occupancy or his boss was breathing fire down his back for higher profits. Or guests were demanding an upgrade to a suite, free gym membership or a free meal. Late check-out or a massive over-booking, he was there for them. He loved them; they were his world. He had said it often.

Doubt clouded Laila's rational mind.

She remembered how as a teenager she had sung, at the top of her voice, "Where Do Broken Hearts Go?" by Whitney Houston. Today she wondered where *do* they go?

Hadn't the *Titanic* been unsinkable? Laila thought miserably. It felt like she had hit an iceberg and was sinking fast.

The wife was always the last to know.

The women who frequented the tennis and golf course or the horse-riding club were having a field day. Laila's husband is having an affair. She got what was coming. She deserved it. Who does she think she is? She saw the thoughts running through their heads whenever she was in a room with them. Just yesterday Pilar and Gabrielle, the wives of the Spanish and Italian ambassadors, had abruptly stopped their conversation at the school gate. Was it her overactive imagination, or were they whispering and sniggering about her? Were they mocking her marriage? The model couple was wobbling on the catwalk.

Laila knew she wasn't popular among the womenfolk. She was pretty, petite, confident and intelligent. Expat women would prefer to see her dressed in traditional Indian wear with *chappals* on her feet, instead of as a modern Indian woman who could stand her own ground. Most were ditzy, more interested in the new lipstick colour at the makeup counter of Muscat Beauty than what was happening in the world.

"I can taste the mossy flavour in this tea."

"I specifically asked for *mineral* water, not *filtered*. Do you understand the difference?"

"A radiologist! Does that mean you're a DJ?"

"We tried this new Chinese restaurant, Saigon, last week. They didn't have the usual spring rolls or wontons or even dim sum."

Flimsy interests in actors from *I'm a Celebrity Get Me Out of Here*, the latest fashion and hair colour, and who wore what at the last diplomatic cocktail party. Locating a country or its capital on a map would be too much for some.

"I wonder how much Pilar's husband earns."

"Does the organisation pay for your house help?"

"Have you been invited to the Russian National Day cocktail?"

"I'm thinking of getting my nose done."

"Ask Violet where she goes for her Botox injections. The guy works wonders."

"Why did you tuck the label of my dress? I want people to see that I can afford this Kenzo dress."

"Ruth's children are badly brought up. That's what you get for leaving them with the maid."

Their days were spent counting who had more house help or social invitations, adding up in their minds to see if their husband earned more. Whose children were cleverer or spoke more languages? You could only speak one language at a time.

"My daughter speaks Chinese," Mandy stated proudly.

So do billions of Chinese, Laila thought. She knew from experience how her language skills were always questioned with 'fluently?'

They thrived on gossip magazines. They only spoke to her because she was the wife of the general manager of the prestigious hotel in Muscat.

But though their company was grating, Laila loved Oman. It was diverse. From the choppy turquoise sea to the rugged mountains. The red-sanded desert and the lush wadis with swaying date palms, luxurious ferns and serpentine lianas. The cleanliness was a far cry from Kinshasa, where rubbish heaps could be found at every corner and potholes were the norm, as were bullet-riddled taxis. The sea of plastic bottles and bags bobbing in the open gutters had been an eyesore. In Muscat, you were fined for driving a dirty vehicle, and it was forbidden to hang out laundry in public view, on main roads or overlooking shopping malls.

Kurt. Kurt. Kurt. Like a thief, he had stolen her heart. The feeling of loving Kurt was like water being pumped into her aorta; she would explode with love for him.

Laila couldn't get her husband out of her mind. How would she broach the subject? Should she be direct? It wasn't as if she could hire a detective like in the movies. Photographs handed over to her in a brown envelope. That would be a laugh.

All Laila's suspicions screamed that something was wrong when Kurt had started going to the gym. He detested working out with a passion. He was more of a sports enthusiast lying on the sofa, remote in hand. He would zap from football to rugby to cricket, knowing the rules of every sport, including curling. He was the exact opposite of Laila, who enjoyed a good game of tennis or golf. His ever-expanding waistline was alarming, and gentle nudging from Laila fell on deaf ears. Kurt enjoyed good food, and in his line of work, it was too easy to fall prey to a decadent chocolate cake, a pan-fried sole, foie gras, lobsters or a rib-eye with béarnaise sauce. He enjoyed bacon rashers for breakfast and a good pork roast at dinner, but red wines were Kurt's weakness. Chateau Cheval Blanc, Chateau Yquem or Chateau Petrus, fine wines he spent a fortune on.

Religiously for the last ten weeks, he'd been up at cock's crow, ready for a thirty-minute run. Getting out of bed was another peeve of his, and now he was literally jumping out without prompting. It was worrying. At 7:00 p.m. he'd be at the hotel gym, lifting weights and doing sit-ups, something he had never done in all their years of marriage. Exercising twice a day? No one in their right mind did that— certainly not her Kurt! He slotted manicures and pedicures into his agenda. How often had Laila coaxed him to take care of his long, tapered hands and feet? He had laughed off her suggestion, pleading no time to waste.

Laila should have taken the bull by the horns immediately when the changes began, but she had slept on her intuition instead of following it. Foolishly, she had thought that Kurt was finally taking care of his physique and his health without prodding from her.

Fear gripped Laila. It was cold and clammy and wrapped its arthritic fingers around her heart. Where would she go? What would she do?

With the birth of Lili, she had given up her job as interior decorator. A job she'd enjoyed after having worked so many years in the hotel industry. The correspondence course had been hard work but she had obtained her diploma with flying colours.

But for the last fifteen years, her life had been dedicated to her family. Colour schemes and fabric swatches had taken a back bench.

Laila loved being a mother. The toughest job in the world had many rewards, and Laila would trade it for nothing in the world. She admired women who juggled work with family life; it had to be doubly hard. Angela Merkel with her four children and a country to run was awe-inspiring. Laila had read in a magazine that she even did her own grocery shopping. She couldn't be that. She needed Kurt. She couldn't do this alone.

Why was she jumping the gun? *You pride yourself on your intelligence. Stop panicking. Stop with your over-active imagination. There must be a perfect explanation for Kurt's behaviour. Pull yourself together*, Laila chided herself while dialling home.

"Laila, my child, is that you?" Lakshmi's sunny voice brought tears to Laila's eyes. Suddenly she missed her mother unbearably.

"Yes, Mummy. How are you?" Laila felt like a two-year-old. *Mummy* was for children; she was an adult with two children of her own. But it felt good. Comforting. Lakshmi would always be her mummy.

"Very well thank you, and how are my granddaughters?"

Laila swallowed the lump in her throat. Should she confide in her mother? All her life, she had been her closest confidant, but Lakshmi loved Kurt dearly. Hearing that her daughter's marriage was rocky would upset her.

The Gulf of Oman was a sparkly blue diamond glittering in the distance. Fishing boats bobbed gently on calm waters. The view was lost on her.

"Laila, are you still there? Are you listening to what I'm saying? Are you okay?"

Laila tried to clear her throat. "I'm fine," came out as a croak. A single tear rolled down her cheek.

"Are you crying, my child? What's the matter? Tell me, Laila," Lakshmi commanded.

Once she got going, Laila couldn't stop. Words tumbled over each other like Niagara Falls. She poured out her heart.

Lakshmi listened, as she always did, without interruption.

"I don't know what to do, Mummy," Laila said, gulping down a sob.

"First, you'll stop crying. It will get you nowhere. Next, you *will* ask Kurt what's going on. Avoiding the matter won't make it better nor will it go away. There could be a good reason for his behaviour. What happened to the strong Laila I know? Where has the fighter in you gone? You won't be the first woman to be cheated on nor will you be the last, but you can't crumple like tissue at the first ripple in your marriage."

"Mummy, is this the best decision?" Laila had composed herself. Conversations with Lakshmi mostly galvanised Laila to be stronger, to want to go further and do better.

"It's the only decision left to you, my child. How long will you keep on wondering what your husband is up to? Do you want to be in the dark? For how long?"

Laila sat upright on the ottoman. Her fighting spirit had come back.

Lakshmi was right; it was the only course left to her. She needed to know who this unfaithful person was. The dimple in her marriage didn't look like a cute little hole; it felt more like an ugly crater. A crater spewing hot lava over her. Where had her kind, gentle, caring Kurt gone?

Laila grabbed her handbag. She would have lunch with Kurt at the hotel. She would ask him calmly. Arguments would have to be kept on a tight rein in the restaurant with staff and guests in close proximity!

Funny, Laila thought. Moira, Kurt's secretary, wasn't at her desk.

She pushed open the door to Kurt's office, then stood still. On reflex, her right hand leapt to her heart. It had stopped beating. Every fibre in her being froze. Is this what death felt like?

Stone cold. Rigor mortis.

Kurt was cradling the face of another man in a passionate embrace. His fingers were entwined in the dark curly hair, the way they had so often entwined in her own.

Laila couldn't move. Her heart that had stopped beating a second ago was now pounding furiously, like a drummer was hammering on it mercilessly. The scream in her throat was lodged tightly, choking her.

Was she dreaming?

Laila blinked involuntarily, just to make sure her vision wasn't deceiving her.

Had she opened the door to the wrong office? But there was no mistaking Kurt. Her Kurt was in the arms of another man. By the looks of it, he was enjoying the intimacy. Feeling as if she was watching herself from outside her skin, Laila forced herself to back quietly out of the office. She stood staring at the oak door. Bewildered. Confused. Hurt. Numb.

Most of all, shocked.

She couldn't breathe. She couldn't think. She couldn't cry. She couldn't move.

"Laila, how are you? Were you playing tennis today?" loquacious Moira asked breezily, arriving back at her desk. "I was with the director of food and beverage. The Diwan is driving us nuts. Are you okay, Laila? You look pale."

Laila took a deep breath. She physically had to pull herself together. She felt like a deep-sea diver who had just come up for air. Her heart was constricting. Was she having a heart attack? She had to get a grip. Did Moira know about Kurt? How she wished that Kurt was having an affair with another woman. Anything would be better than her husband preferring a man to her.

A punch in the gut couldn't begin to cover the way she felt. Her ego was being battered like a carpet hung out for cleaning the old-fashioned way. *Thump! Thump! Thump!* The huge, rounded, wooden stick kept slamming all over her body. Was this how Mike Tyson's opponent felt after a couple of rounds in the ring?

Concentrate, Laila told herself. Even if it was only for the sake of appearances. She couldn't—no, wouldn't—break down in front of Moira.

"I left Kurt in a meeting with the personal assistant of the Royal Diwan. I'll just buzz him that you're here," Moira said, in her bubbly way.

Kurt's tastes seemed to lean toward personal assistants, Laila thought bitterly.

"Listen, Moira, I didn't realise the time. I have a facial in a while. Please don't disturb Kurt; I'll see him this evening."

Laila almost fell over in her rush to get out of the office, which seemed far too small and confining.

She needed to get away. She needed to compose herself. She needed time to think. How would she face Kurt this evening? Would she be able to act normally? Should she confront him? How *could* he? Where had she gone wrong? Wasn't their marriage the perfect one? Kurt was the love of her life. Her world. The words *no* and *why* kept turning over and over in her mind. Was she at fault? Had she missed the signs? Was she a bad wife? A bad lover?

Her marriage was solid as a rock. How many times had she told herself that?

The scene of Kurt in another man's arms kept playing over and over in her mind. Every time she shut her eyes she saw them. The passion. The yearning. The tenderness. Everything that she'd believed she had in her marriage. What happened to their yin-and-yang relationship that she treasured?

It was earth-shattering.

Laila felt weak. All she wanted was to curl up and die.

Her world had stopped turning. It was on a collision course with all the planets in the universe. She needed to be alone. Gather her thoughts. She told Anwar the driver to drop her off at the Corniche. The walk along the beach would do her good. Could the sea breeze clear her head? Put things in perspective after her rollercoaster plunge?

She had always thought that their relationship was like fireworks: sparkly, vivid, intense and beautiful. Right now, like all fireworks, it was fizzling out rapidly.

A mistress, even two, would have been preferable.

Laila took off her sandals and hoisted her skirt. The fine white sand sifted through her toes as she dug her feet into the warm Gulf of Oman waters. Overcome with anger, she shouted out to God.

"Why? Why me? What have I ever done to you? Have I not been a faithful servant?"

The waves lapped at her ankles. There was no response to her angry questions from the heavens above, only the sun blazing down Laila's neck, almost mocking her grief in its intensity.

The evening dragged. Laila knew she was testy with Lili and Lalita, who didn't deserve the irritated answers to their innocent everyday questions. She tried to curb her anger. How many times had she glanced at her wristwatch since returning from the beach? She couldn't wait for bedtime. Tonight, there'd be no tickling nor storytelling.

"Aren't you going to read us a story mama?" Lalita asked, her little head just visible under the *Pocahontas* sheet.

"Not tonight," Laila muttered, snapping the light switch off.

She stood for several seconds outside the door, trying to calm down. She knew she couldn't hang around the corridor the entire evening.

"You were awfully silent tonight. Something bothering you, Laila?"

Laila stared at the man she didn't recognise anymore. Should she tell him, or would it be better if he told her in his own time? Laila had played conversation openers over and over in her aching mind. She had thought about nothing else the entire afternoon. The sea air hadn't brought clarity. The choppy waters, the salty air and her rant at the Almighty had only made her headache worse. She had popped two painkillers into her mouth the minute she got back.

Her well-rehearsed speech was of no use. Laila felt tongue-tied. Her mouth was dry, and breathing had become difficult. It had been impossible to eat. All she could think about was the image of Kurt in another man's arms chiselled in stone in her mind.

Her Kurt with another man.

She had noticed the girls giving each other the eye during dinner. They knew something wasn't right with their parents. They were as close as two peas in a pod with only eighteen months between them. Laila was sure that as they shared a room they talked about their parents among other things, especially the recent rift.

"Moira told me you passed by at lunchtime. Why did you rush off? We could have eaten together. I didn't know you had a facial. You had one last week." Kurt looked at Laila quizzically.

The weight loss suited him. He had a commanding physique with his broad shoulders.

Laila kept silent. Letting the perfect opportunity slip by. She couldn't mouth the words. Even eye contact was near impossible.

"Laila, will you talk to me? What is the matter with you?" Kurt sat on the edge of the bed, his leg touching Laila's.

Laila moved like she had been burnt.

"Hey, can't I sit next to my wife?"

Laila stared at Kurt. How could he pretend nothing was wrong? He was cheating on her—with a man! Nothing could be worse.

Anger had been replaced by hurt, the only emotion that surged through Laila's body as she sat beside her husband.

"Do you have anything to say to me, Kurt?" The bold side of her couldn't stand not knowing. She needed answers.

"What would I want to say, Laila? You're talking in riddles tonight." A frown creased Kurt's forehead.

Laila stood and walked to the window. It was dark outside. The lights of downtown Muscat flickered in the distance. Laila could make out the red neon sign of KFC, the bulb in the C burnt.

If only Kurt would come clean and make this easier. She didn't want to broach the subject. If Kurt wouldn't open up to her, she had no choice but to take the bull by the horns, however badly she would be gored.

"I saw you, Kurt," she said softly.

"What do you mean, saw me? Where? Today?" Kurt looked baffled. "You're still talking in riddles, Laila."

"In your office with the PA of the Diwan."

The silence stretched, and Laila wondered if she had said it to herself. She turned around to find Kurt sitting perfectly still, his head slightly bowed.

"Kurt?"

He raised his head slowly and stared at Laila with haunted, bloodshot eyes. The transformation from a few minutes ago was incredible. Kurt looked worn out, old. He shook his head from side to side, like he was trying to clear it. Or was he trying to deny to himself what Laila had seen?

Laila didn't know how long they waited in silence. Both afraid of what lay ahead.

"Laila." Kurt stopped, then repeated Laila's name again.

"Kurt, why?" The pain and hurt in Laila was raw. Her shoulders stooped, and her brow furrowed. She steadied the tremble in her voice and continued, "You're gay? How long has this been going on? Do I need to get tested for HIV? Is this an experiment or have you always leaned toward that side? Why, Kurt? Why?"

"Laila. Please. I never meant for you to find out like this."

"Did you ever want me to find out? Can you imagine how I felt seeing you in the arms of another *man*? Of all the things that have been running through my head the last few months, this was the last thing I expected. Has our marriage been a sham, Kurt? What do I tell our daughters?"

"You can't tell them." Kurt raised his voice. In a calmer voice, "Not now, please."

"They deserve an explanation. I deserve one too. What kind of relationship are we looking at? You can't ask for my silence."

"I need time, Laila. For now, all I can tell you is that I do love you."

Laila laughed mirthlessly. "Do you also love the PA of the Royal Diwan?

"Please believe me, Laila. I never stopped loving you and I never will. You're beautiful. You're a wonderful, kind, generous, intelligent woman."

"Stop, Kurt. I can't hear you say such things after this afternoon. You painted a different picture. I don't know if I'll ever believe you. It's too painful. Too hurtful. You've broken my heart."

Laila couldn't believe the calm she was capable of. The roiling seas of this afternoon had turned the tide. Had her brain gone into meltdown or was it her heart? The hurt, disgust and fury had turned into utter sadness and a deep, deep void. Her ego and confidence had taken a tumble. Would she ever recover?

"I never, ever wanted to hurt you or our daughters. You have to believe me."

"Which Kurt is the real one? You or the one I saw this afternoon? Have you always had homosexual leanings?"

"No. I don't know. Maybe."

"Which one is it, Kurt?" Laila snapped.

She felt she would break in half. Kurt was standing close behind her. She had the urge to lean her head against his shoulder. How wonderful it would be to be comforted by her husband of eighteen years. She longed to hear that she was mistaken. That she was dreaming. She would awaken and everything would go back to yesterday.

It was not a dream.

She couldn't trust him. Not with her bleeding heart and not with the hurting she was going through. She hadn't the courage to call Lakshmi. How would she explain to her mother? No matter how broad-minded Lakshmi and Amit were, homosexuality didn't bode well in Indian society. It was taboo.

She would have to get tested for HIV. They were in Oman, a country that claimed that there were no cases of AIDS.

"I can't do this anymore, Kurt. I'm tired. My brain and body are exhausted."

Kurt didn't argue. He looked at Laila helplessly, silently stepping back. Sleep was the last thing on Laila's mind, but it was an excuse. An escape from today. She was bone-weary. Monosyllabic answers from Kurt weren't enough. She had sprung a surprise on him, but she was the one who'd had to deal with an even bigger surprise in her relationship. Even a string of women would have been better than this!

Death, even.

As Laila turned, Kurt grabbed her hand. "Believe me, hurting you was the last thing I wanted. I *do* love you, Laila."

Laila looked into Kurt's blue eyes. They were filled with tears. The look was tortured and haunted.

She couldn't stop loving him. He was the father of their children. No matter what his transgressions—and there were many today—he had given her two beautiful, intelligent and kind daughters. She shouldn't feel sympathy for him, but she did in an odd way.

She withdrew her hand slowly from Kurt's clasp. "We'll talk tomorrow."

She was angry with Kurt, but it was better this way. Why hurl mean insults that she would regret in the morning? They both deserved kindness tonight.

What lay ahead? Would Kurt come out? Would they get through this?

She had believed that Kurt, her Kurt, was having an affair. A pregnant mistress would have been better news. Laila laughed hollowly. If he had said that, she would have been furious. She would have probably hurled something at him.

She had fallen face-first into the sewer, grappling in the shit. It was gagging her, making her sick. It was oozing out of every pore of her being. Laila swallowed hard. There was no getting rid of the nausea. She barely made it to the bathroom sink before she threw up the little dinner she had eaten. She splashed water over her clammy cheeks and rinsed her mouth out with Listerine.

It was August, peak summer. Both taps gushed hot water even with the geyser off. She felt dirty.

Laila lowered herself into the steaming bath water. Almost scalded her skin. She shook her head involuntary. When had he found time to take another man as a lover? With the hotel running on full occupancy, the seminars, conferences, ever-growing mound of paperwork, their constant social calendar and Royal Diwan functions.

Royal Diwan functions. That was it. Laila couldn't stop shaking. Reality was sinking in. Kurt hadn't even tried to deny her accusations. There wasn't much to deny, but how she had willed him to try. To say it was an experiment, a spur of the moment thing. A mid-life crisis.

Her world was suddenly spinning in the opposite direction.

Why would Kurt ruin their happy marriage?

Weren't they the perfect couple?

Hurt turned into rage, rushing like champagne bubbles straight to her head. She closed her eyes for a few seconds, breathing in deeply, willing herself to calm down.

Calm was not what she felt. She felt revulsion. She felt used and stupid. A hundred different ways of hurting Kurt were running through her brain. She had loved him blindly. Never complained, nor questioned the move to a different country every two to three years. Had stuck by him. Supporting him through thick and thin. Being his right hand. The left had slapped her full in the face, like a perfect backhand.

They could discuss anything, from religion to politics to music, with passion. She would, just for the heck of it, take the exact opposite of Kurt's opinion. It was a running joke for them. She would be brown and he would be white. Kurt had never wanted someone who smiled and agreed with whatever he said, like the majority of women she met during her travels.

Their lovemaking had always been great. But the days of Kurt waking her up in the middle of the night had dwindled. She used to feel flattered that he wanted her at 3:00 a.m., but though he didn't wake her up anymore, he still managed to leave her gasping for breath.

Laila padded softly into the bedroom. Kurt was lying on the bed, staring at the ceiling. He looked old and broken. Her heart ached. *You can't stop love*, she thought bitterly.

Be kind, Laila told herself, even though she wanted to throw him out of the bedroom. He could sleep on the sofa or get a room in the hotel—he had the master key! But the girls would notice, and Laila didn't want her daughters to be distraught.

She took a deep breath and lay down next to her husband. Kurt didn't talk or approach her. For the first time in eighteen years, they didn't sleep entwined.

Laila slept fitfully. Kurt's tossing and turning told her he wasn't sleeping either.

She woke up with a throbbing headache. It was going to be a long and painful day. The relentless Omani heat created a suffocating haze in the early morning air.

Lili and Lalita were dressed and ready for school without any prompting from Laila.

"Are you okay, Ma?" Lili looked worried. She was fourteen, but wise for her age. Sometimes Laila felt guilty for speaking to her like an adult. Even at barely eighteen months, Laila would leave her to watch over Lalita while she rushed for a shower or cooked a meal, or cleaned after housekeeping as their way wasn't as meticulous as hers. The perfectionist in Laila related well to Bree from *Desperate Housewives*.

Lalita hadn't spoken until she was three years of age. No *Ma-ma* or *Pa-pa*. No sounds. Laila had been sure she was deaf. Lili would say what Lalita wanted to eat or wear or what toy she wanted to play with. The paediatrician explained that Lili was her decoder, and that was why she made no effort to speak. She would speak when she felt the absolute need. When Lalita had started to talk at the age of three, it had been in whole sentences. After that, they couldn't shut her up.

"I'm fine, sweetie," Laila said. "Stop worrying."

"Are you and Dad talking?"

Silence, the worse punishment!

"Yes, we are, Lili. I told you, stop worrying. Everything will be fine."

It hurt her to lie. She didn't know whether things would be fine. Her life was in limbo. She shouldn't be abrupt with Lili. The girls needed answers too. It was just that right now, she didn't have any.

She hugged Lili for a second. "I promise I'll let you know if something is wrong, my Lili."

All Laila wanted was for the girls to be off to school.

Kurt had been in front of the computer when she entered the dining room. He had avoided eye contact. Laila wanted answers. Her weariness had now been replaced by anger. She'd been caught in the fluctuation from anger to hurt since yesterday. A pendulum—hurt, anger, anger, hurt.

Laila felt bereft and empty. Like someone close to her had died.

She handed the girls their lunchboxes and kissed them on the forehead.

"Have a good day, my darlings. Work hard."

Lalita hugged Laila tight. Kindred spirits. "Don't be sad, Mama."

Laila swallowed the lump. She wouldn't cry. Not in front of the girls.

"Where did you get that silly idea from, Lali?"

Lalita shrugged. Laila stood on the front doorstep, and Lili squeezed her hand on her way to the car.

When Kurt walked past, she said, "We need to talk. Can you come back after you drop off the girls?" The French school wasn't far from the villa. He would be back within twenty minutes.

Kurt nodded. Still no eye contact.

She waited until the car had driven off before going back inside.

***

"I need to know, Kurt, have you always been gay? And why have you never come clean?"

They were sitting opposite each other at the dining table. Laila had given the maid the day off so they could be alone. The cream linen tablecloth had been ironed to perfection. The flower arrangement of lilies and gardenia wafted in the air, the two scents Laila loved.

Kurt sighed. Finally, he raised his eyes to Laila.

"I don't know, Laila. I do know that I was attracted to you. There was chemistry between us. But..."

Silence stretched.

Laila didn't know how to react, so she stayed mum.

Finally, Kurt continued. "My father was a hard man. He permanently put me down. He said often he didn't want a sissy for a son. All my life I tried to please him. In the beginning, I would run to my mum for comfort until he forbade that. He ruled the house with an iron fist. We were Christian, it was frowned upon. If you were gay, that meant there was something wrong with you. You needed prayers, you needed to pray for forgiveness, and you needed to fit in with society. I tried hard to live up to my father's expectations of me. Being gay was definitely not one of them. My sisters married early just to get away from him and his obsession with God."

Kurt clumsily reached for Laila's hand, like a blind man. Laila didn't want his touch. The wound was open and raw. How long would it take her to get over this feeling of betrayal?

"Laila, I never meant to betray nor hurt you. Believe me. I do love you. You and the girls are my life."

Kurt stared at her, a broken man. The circles under his eyes were dark as bruises.

They had been each other's rocks for eighteen years. They had supported each other through thick and thin. Moving every couple of years was never easy. New places. New people. New experiences. New friends. New cultures. New bosses. But through it all, they had each other.

"Where do we go from here, Kurt? What do we tell the girls? Divorce the next step?"

"No!" Kurt raised his voice. He pushed back the chair and ran a hand through his hair. An action Laila recognised whenever he was stressed. His chestnut hair flopped back down. "No, Laila, please."

"Kurt you *cannot* have your cake and eat it too. What kind of a relationship are we hanging on to?"

"The best relationship that I know of. Better than any other I know."

"I can't live a lie, Kurt. The girls deserve the truth." Hazel eyes locked with blue ones.

"Laila, I realise I don't deserve any sympathy or understanding from you. Not after what I've put you through. Not after yesterday. I've been a fool. I was selfish. No, not was—I *am* selfish." Kurt looked beseechingly at Laila.

You can't stop loving. Love wasn't a tap that you could turn on and off. Yes, she was hurting, but so was Kurt. It couldn't be easy for him. She couldn't un-know her husband because the situation suited her.

"The more things change, Laila, the more they stay the same. We're no longer in the eighties, but homosexuality is frowned upon in the company, and more so here in the Middle East. I don't want to risk losing my job. Most of all, I don't want to lose you or my precious daughters. I promise I won't bring my other life home ever. We can stay together. At least until the girls are old enough to understand. Can we try? I don't want you to leave. Please?"

Laila stared long and hard at Kurt. Who was this man? Was this a trick to keep her in his life? He loved his daughters that much, Laila was sure of. No one could act to that extent, not even Meryl Streep.

What was she to do? Laila was even more confused. She was silent for a long time, trying to come to the best decision for her daughters and herself. Could they keep on living as husband and wife in name only for the sake of Kurt's job and, more importantly, for her family? The transition for the girls would be easier when they were older and better able to understand sexual orientation. It would make life easier on the financial front, that much Laila knew.

She was unsure whether her decision was selfish or selfless.

"Alright, Kurt, we'll do it your way. I can't believe I'm doing this. Don't get too excited. It's just for now. Until I decide what to do next. For the girls." Laila spoke softly but clearly. She didn't know whether it was a good decision, but it would have to do for now.

Time would tell.

"Thank you, Laila."

"I don't care what you do, Kurt, but you'll be absolutely discreet. If the girls ever find out the way I did, I'll personally kill you."

Kurt nodded. "I promise. It will never ever come to that. I'm truly, truly sorry, Laila."

Laila went into the bedroom and shut the door. She stood still for a long time. Had she made the right decision? From now on, she would have to pretend to the outside world that she was in a happy marriage. How would she pull the wool over her precious daughters' eyes? They were intelligent girls.

She was exhausted. Every bone in her body hurt, every nerve shouted for release from the tension and heartbreak. Sitting on the ottoman, she wept. It felt good to vent out the hurt, betrayal and loss in tears.

She hadn't called Lakshmi again. She wouldn't, couldn't tell her.

Secrets. How many would she have to keep in the months and years to come?

Would she be capable of keeping up the charade with Kurt? Could they live under the same roof without any animosity, without the girls suspecting that things had changed between their parents?

"One day at a time," Laila whispered.

She had to get back in the saddle, steer her life back on course. Think of the future. Plan. Eighteen years of marriage had come to an end. It was like death. She needed to bury her relationship, mourn and grieve. Come to terms with the loss.

The familiar ring of the phone in the hall jostled Laila back to earth. Caller ID told her it was Lakshmi. How long could she avoid her mother? What would she tell her? What story could she cook up?

"Laila, my child, are you avoiding me?"

"Why would I do that, Ma?" Laila made her voice as sunny as possible.

"Did you speak to Kurt?"

"I did, and he firmly denied an affair with a woman. He claims I have an overactive imagination working overtime. It's all good, Ma."

She was telling the truth. Kurt wasn't having an affair with a woman.

"And you believe him? Are you sure, Laila? Are you hiding something from me, my child?"

Secrets and lies. She was behaving like her aunts Myla and Kavita. Laila prayed she would be able to keep up with the lies.

"I promise you I'm fine. We had a long talk, and Kurt has assured me. He was caught up with work. I shouldn't have doubted him, Ma."

However broad-minded Lakshmi was, Laila knew that homosexuality was taboo. It was too delicate a subject. For all Lakshmi's prayers, it would need a miracle to turn things around. It wasn't an adolescent experiment that her Kurt was going through.

"I'm glad, Laila. Divorce is an ugly matter."

"I know, Ma. Believe me, I'm fine," Laila lied.

Would that ever be true? As with everything, time would tell.

***

The HIV test came out negative. A relief. The young Indian doctor didn't ask questions, just silently drew Laila's blood. Face blank. Laila felt like her spirit was being drained with her blood, leaving her weak and utterly sad.

Recovery would take time. Was there a biopsy that could be done for an aching heart? Was there a cure?

In public, Laila and Kurt behaved like any other happy, very-much-in-love couple. Still holding hands and laughing at all the right times. In the beginning, it had been hard and conversation stilted. They jumped the hurdle together. Practice does make perfect. The girls were happy that their parents were happy again.

Some days, Laila cried on her own. She missed her husband. She missed her old life. Kurt had apologised incessantly until Laila had begged him to stop. The relationship had shifted from being lovers. They were even better friends, if that could be possible.

Time was what they needed. Time was what Laila would give herself and her precious family. Love knows no bounds. Like the Japanese art of *kintsugi*, she would fix the broken pot with rivulets of gold until the day she came clean to her daughters and found her own wings to fly.

CHAPTER 8

"MELTING POT"

November 2002

Audrey managed once again to find a way of getting under Laila's skin. Try as Laila did to be amicable, she was a difficult person to like.

Why did she still play tennis with her? she wondered distractedly as she scrubbed the kitchen counter.

Her obsession with cleanliness was growing with each passing day. Her compulsion to scrupulously wash her hands after touching anything, wipe down tins and cans, take several showers a day, count the stairs and the meatballs she cooked was part of Laila's routine. The urge to straighten picture frames, whether in the corridors of the hotel or in public. Stray hairs, even on the floor, made Laila shudder. Toilets and bathrooms had to gleam. She inspected the apartment minutely after housekeeping every day. Her obsession bordered on panic attacks when she was in unclean environments. Laila would sit stiffly, praying she wouldn't require the loo. She joked with Kurt that some places they were invited to should require a mandatory cholera vaccine before crossing the threshold.

Dust balls, clumps of hair, cobwebs that would do justice on a Halloween set, grimy skirting boards, food crumbs and animal fur were visible. Clothes draped over furniture or tossed under the bed, and toys and other paraphernalia scattered across the living room floor. Dirty windows and sticky light switches. The unidentifiable layer on the TV remote control, the ring of grime in the bath tub, or the hob and surrounding area covered in grease was equivalent to watching a horror movie for Laila.

"Didn't they notice the state of the toilet before it got so bad?" Laila had asked, turning her head away from the telly. "I can't bear these adverts for toilet and bathroom products!"

"Are you actually closing your eyes? You're funny, Ma," Lili said, shaking her dark curls.

Laila's handbags held several sanitisers, room sprays and wet wipes. She didn't see this as an obsession. She was clean; that's how she explained it to her family.

Laila looked at her dry cuticles, the result of constant use of water. She applied another layer of lotion.

Audrey had left a tiny flat in Paris to come to paradise in Dubai. She and her family had given up the rat race of Metro, Boulot, Dodo—commute, work, sleep—for a luxurious villa, a chauffeur, a maid, two gardeners and a cook. The perks had gone to her head. The chauffeur had body odour, the maid was incompetent, the gardeners didn't know the difference between a weed and a blade of grass, and she could whip up a better meal than the cook! Why she still held on to her staff was beyond Laila.

Shouldn't she return home if she was so unhappy in Dubai? Air France had daily flights to Paris. She could go back to cleaning her own toilet, driving in traffic in the twelfth arrondissement, cooking her own meals, taking public transport, paying taxes and dealing with monthly transportation and factory strikes. She had the gall to moan the three days it rained in Dubai! How did she deal with the rain five days out of seven in Paris?

She spoke zee English with zee French accente, of course; nothing adorable about it.

"Do you even know what zee quiche is, Laila?"

Laila feigned ignorance. It made Audrey happy to feel superior. *Whatever floats her boat*, Laila thought.

She had met many Audreys during her travels. Expats who thought that, as they were in a developing country, they were better than the locals. Africans were stupid, Indians were corrupt, Chinese were dirty, and Arabs were lazy.

"Why so many of you people in Dubai?"

"So many of *you* people also," Laila retorted, her patience wearing thin.

The twice-weekly game of tennis was played in a skimpy skirt. Audrey loped from one side of the court to the other with full accessories, long blonde hair bouncing in the Arabian winds in time with the cellulite on her thighs.

"Have you noticed the size of the diamond ring?" Kathleen, Laila's doubles partner, nudged her.

"Fake, most probably. It looks heavier than the racquet!"

"Like the lashes, this morning."

Kathleen and Laila shared a knowing smile before Laila readied to serve.

After a game, the conversation always reverted to the incompetence of the people, be they Indian, Egyptian, Vietnamese or South African. The French, it seemed, were the only capable folk. Didn't Francois Hollande prove that?

Audrey's husband worked on a drill at Shell. In conversation she made it sound like Shell would grind to a halt if he wasn't holding the rig! Her children were tiny clones of their mother. They mimicked her behaviour, which was natural. Why shouldn't they throw clothes, the school bag, food and toys at the maid? She was the stupid Indian servant. It was her job to pick up after them. She was paid for it.

Laila wondered if the shoe was on the other foot, would Audrey and her family be content with this treatment?

The morning game had ended with Audrey recounting her weekend escapades as usual. Today it was a picnic with her family in a wadi in the Wahiba Sands. The group of ladies had listened, first in amazement, then in disbelief.

"Zee heat was terrible, *mais vraiment* terrible. Thank God zee gardener and zee maid come with us. Zhey cut the branches of the palm trees to make zee air for my children, my husband and myself. Zhey stand outside for one hour when we eat. Otherwise, how we eat with so hot weather? The parasol is not enough from zee hot sun. This very good *idee* from me, no?"

"No," Laila snapped, resisting the urge to scream it out. Why was Audrey so dense to the feelings of others? Her lack of empathy knew no bounds.

"You didn't really make them do that?" politically-correct Olivia asked, baffled.

"*Mais* of course! I pay them. Why zhey can't make zee air for me?"

172

"You can't make your house help fan you. We're not living in the time of Tutankhamun?" Olivia tried reasoning.

"Who tutan-person?" Without pausing for breath, Audrey continued, ignoring Olivia, who was still uncomprehending. "Don't forget zee coffee on Wednesday at ten a.m."

She had repeated the sentence to Laila and the other ladies five times in total since they had begun the game.

"Laila, can I ask zee favour of you?"

Laila raised her eyebrows, wondering what 'the slave-driver' wanted.

"Could you bring zee samosas for tomorrow?"

What happened to your fantastic culinary skills and your full-time cook? Instead, Laila asked sweetly, "Would you like me to bring zee waiter as well?"

The sarcasm was lost on Audrey, who strode off not bothered by Laila's comment.

Why did Laila attract such people? Why were they faze-proof? Urvashi had the same hippo-like hide, years ago.

The way Audrey had insisted on her coffee morning, Laila had expected nothing less than high tea, Fortnum and Mason style. What Audrey produced was a plate of supermarket ginger cookies and weak Lipton tea in a kitsch environment. There was no offer of coffee or even a fruit juice. The other ladies had all been asked to bring a dish as well. They obediently did so.

"Bring a dish or bottle" were parties Laila preferred to decline. It started off with a dish—why stop there? Why not saucepans, televisions, fridges or even a car for a housewarming, hen night or wedding?

Laila was itching to show Audrey how to have a real coffee morning. Catering wouldn't pose a problem; she was 'married' to an hotelier.

All's fair in love and war.

***

D-Day arrived. The executive chef had prepared a sumptuous buffet worthy of even a seven-star hotel. Chicken, meat and vegetable samosas in silver chafing dishes; Audrey would be pleased. Buttery chicken vol-au-vent, salmon sandwiches, duck spring rolls, morel and leek quiches, foie gras canapes, sweet and sour king prawns, crab patties, crepe Suzette, an avocado and mango cheesecake, cupcakes with fluffy lime and mint icing, pain-au-chocolat, croissants, Danish pastries, freshly squeezed juices from ordinary orange to exotic mangosteen and kiwi. Tattinger champagne in fluted glasses, oolong tea and Ethiopian coffee. It was a spread fit for a queen!

The view from the glass rooftop restaurant of the hotel was impressive. A bird's eye view of Dubai city. The infrastructure of flyovers, side roads, alleys and highways intertwined like tangled tagliatelle. Immaculate flower beds and majestic palms added splashes of colour along streets and roundabouts. Vertiginous skyscrapers fought for space with apartment blocks. Sunlight bounced off dazzling tinted windows, with the Arabian Sea glimmering and glittering like a thousand diamonds in the distance.

The ladies knew Laila's husband worked in the hotel, but as she'd been vague, no one was sure if he worked in finance or food and beverage. Audrey was a woman on a mission, determined to have Kurt's letter of appointment as proof of his position. Laila ignored her prying question three times. Finally, when she demanded for the fourth time, Laila snapped, "Actually he's the general manager."

Audrey was caught off guard and stunned into silence, which was a welcome respite.

"What school do your daughters go to?" Kathleen asked Laila.

Kathleen had left Ireland twenty years ago; Dubai was home for her. She haggled in the souks like a true Emirati, having perfected Arabic. She was warm and hilarious; Laila enjoyed her dry sense of humour.

"The French School."

"How come you chose the French School? Usually, expatriates opt for the British or American system. You didn't consider the madrasa?" Kathleen said, tongue in cheek as she referred to the Arabic school.

Laila laughed. "Kurt is French but was brought up in England. He's English in many ways but he wanted his daughters to have a French education."

"I knew it, I knew it. I just *knew* zhat zee general manager of this hotel couldn't be an Indian!"

Laila stared at Audrey's triumphant look. She was actually gloating over her discovery.

Who did she think ran the most luxurious palaces in India? Places that were sought by presidents, royalty, the super-rich and famous? High-ranking positions are not only for white expatriates. What century was Audrey living in?

"Why? Are Indians incapable of running hotels?" Laila asked quietly. She smiled, even though she could have gladly wrung Audrey's neck. She wouldn't let her spoil her morning.

It dawned on Audrey that she had made a faux pas. Her triumphant look was replaced by embarrassment. "I didn't mean it like zhat. Really."

Laila continued to smile pleasantly. "There's no need to explain. I got your point. It's a free world after all. We're all allowed our opinions. *N'est-ce pas*?"

Audrey was squirming in her seat. Laila hoped in future, she would have filters when she spoke and not blurt out the first thing that came to mind. The other ladies were uncomfortable. Laila tried to fill the potent silence with small talk, but even witty Kathleen had nothing to say. The sound of cutlery against crockery was deafening at the other tables in the restaurant. The piped music sounded like a discotheque. The food wasn't as exquisite as it had been a few minutes ago and the panoramic view was wasted, as the design on the jacquard tablecloth looked more interesting.

"I'm so sorry, Laila. Marie-Antoinette ruined your lovely morning," Kathleen whispered in Laila's ear.

Laila laughed, then brushed her apologies aside. "No problem, Kathleen. I'm glad you could come."

Audrey made a quick exit after that.

Laila couldn't wait for the evening—she would have lots to tell Kurt. They had left Oman a few months ago, and their strained relationship was now on smooth ground. They still slept in the same bed but without lovemaking. She missed it. Many mornings, Laila woke up in Kurt's arms. The girls were still in the dark about their father, but as a family, they were close.

Laila had decided to go back to work part-time. The girls didn't need her as much, and she needed to keep her mind occupied. She threw herself into the interior design world, and the confidence that Kurt had taken away from her with his sexual preference she gained tenfold in working again. She came in contact with elite Emirati families willing to pay a good price for a 'French' decorator. Two afternoons a week, she gave French lessons to Sultana, the wife of an extremely wealthy businessman who dabbled in diamonds, oil, hotels and cars. She seemed to live in another world.

"Why I need to buy air ticket, Laaaila? My husband has private plane."

"Go shopping? Never, Laaaila. Harrods, Saks or Printemps send their people to my hotel suite."

"Book a table in a restaurant? La, la, la," she said, waving a slim finger. "The chef will come to the suite to cook for us, Laila, or my husband will call and they will close the restaurant for us!"

Sultana would click her tongue in exasperation like Laila couldn't understand such simple things.

"Let's have tea, Laaaila, and watch Amitabh Bachchan on DVD." Like Laila, Sultana was an avid fan of Bollywood.

Laila's refusal to accept extra money was met with eye-rolling and tutting from Sultana. On Laila's birthday, she received the familiar blue Tiffany box with the most exquisite pear-drop diamond earrings. When she blurted that it was too much, she couldn't accept such an extravagant present, Sultana replied, "Laaaila, you very silly girl. What mean extravagant? This very small gift. My husband buy these kind of earrings, maybe fifty, every time he go New York. You like, very good. You keep. Now no more talk, okay?"

Dubai was a buzzing city.

Church bells tolled on Sundays at the same time as the muezzin called for prayer. It was a giant melting pot of cultures and religions. The people were as diverse as the cuisines, fashion and languages that fused to make it the metropolis that it was.

It was far too bustling for Laila. She'd preferred the quieter life that Muscat offered. The Omanis were staid, pleasant and humble. Laila missed seeing Omani women with their colourful kaftans and black and gold masks for their eyes bargaining in Muttrah Souk, the smell of ground cardamom wafting the tiny alleys, a pot of thick green coffee readily offered to customers. Omani men in cream, blue and black gallabiyahs, intricately hand-embroidered turbans of different colours on their heads and sandals on their feet, talking animatedly, whittled neem sticks in their mouths.

Emiratis were dapper and flamboyant in comparison. The men with their perfectly trimmed beards and dazzling white gallabiyahs and red and white keffiyehs, leather shoes shining. The women in black, floating, bejewelled abayas, beehive headscarves and flawless makeup with elaborate kohl around almond eyes. Eyebrows were perfectly threaded or tattooed. The woody smell of frankincense was replaced by the heady, sickeningly sweet smell of oud.

Since the coffee morning, many expat wives had been even friendlier to Laila. Audrey lay low and smiled and nodded in Laila's direction but nothing further. Initially, she'd gushed over Laila in an effort to redeem herself, but Laila put a distance between them. She refused Audrey's invitations to afternoon tea, ladies' lunches, casual drinks and dinners. Why did she want an Indian friend?

The constant moaning and criticising wasn't what she had come to a foreign country for. She preferred to browse in the antique silver and gold souks, wadi bash with her family in the desert, interact with local women making a living from weaving baskets or wool carpets, or visit a date plantation.

It was better to sift the wheat from the chaff. Sometimes in life there had to be hierarchy; you just couldn't be friends with everyone or anyone.

***

While in Dubai, Laila helped Manu, a housekeeping employee, with English classes.

He stood shyly at the door. He had on his best clothes. The shoes shone but were two sizes too big for him. He had borrowed them. He was honoured that the wife of the big boss had given up her time to teach him to read and write, *and* in her apartment! He had been working as a gardener for the landscaping company but hadn't been paid his salary of fifty dollars a month in over six months. He shared a container with eighteen to twenty other men from Nepal, where he came from, or Pakistan.

"Please, sir. I need job in hotel. Please, help me," Manu had said when he first came here, dropping to his knees. It had taken all his courage to speak to the general manager.

He had accosted Kurt while he was doing the rounds of the prestigious resort hotel in Bahrain, and Kurt didn't know how to react.

"Stand up, please."

Kindness had won. Kurt had asked the executive housekeeper to put Manu in training for room steward.

Manu's joy was boundless. He had become an avid student, learning quickly how to make up a bed, clean a bathroom, dust, vacuum and mop. His life had turned around. His crowded bunker had been exchanged for a room shared with only two other employees. There was a sitting room with a television, a fully equipped kitchen, a washing machine, *and* he could eat three meals a day at the staff cafeteria. His salary was over five times what he had earned as a gardener. Pittance, perhaps, in the western world, but a fortune for Manu.

"Remember the gardener I was telling you about, Laila? I understand from the housekeeper that he's illiterate."

"Really? I could teach him," Laila said hesitantly.

She had time on her hands, and this was better than spending it in front of the telly, zapping from one channel to another out of three hundred.

Why was it that the more satellite channels there are, the less there was to watch? Reality shows were not Laila's cup of tea. Watching *The Kardashians? Back to Amish? Sex sent me to the ER? Botched? My 600-lb Life? Tiaras and Toddlers? Desperate Miami Housewives? WAGs?*

Truth be told, Laila had a weakness for Zee Television and Zee World. Hindi movies and series were watched regularly and avidly. The scenery was breathtaking, as were the costumes and jewellery. Laila lamented the lack of "happily ever after" in many Indian movies. Why was love unrequited in this part of the world?

When Manu arrived for his first lesson, he wouldn't meet her eyes.

"Why are you standing there, Manu? Come in, please."

Manu removed his shoes.

"Leave your shoes on," Laila said, smiling.

Manu entered timidly, eyes lowered as was custom in eastern culture. His English was broken, but he spoke Arabic rather well.

"*Shukran*. Thank you, madam, for teaching me." He bent to touch Laila's feet.

"No need for that, Manu." Laila stepped back in embarrassment.

The books she had bought that morning lay on the dining table. One first-grade alphabet book and one book on how to write the alphabet and numbers. Manu caressed the books. He put them to his nose and sniffed the new smell. His eyes lit up.

"I've covered the books for you, Manu, so they remain clean."

He nodded enthusiastically. He touched the colouring pencils, sharpener and rubber, reverently.

With no teaching experience, Laila taught Manu the way she had Lili and Lalita years ago. He was a fast learner, and Laila was proud of her accomplishments and those of her student. She wondered who looked forward to the bi-weekly sessions more.

"Do you have children, Manu?"

"I had a daughter. She six months, very sick. My wife ask for like one dollar to go doctor, but I work in garden; no money. She die."

Laila swallowed hard, forcing tears away. One dollar! Life wasn't fair. Why did some have enough to overdose on drugs while others didn't have a dollar to buy necessary drugs?

"Why madam sad? I have more children after. God very good. In my village, I am big man now, working in hotel!" Manu's chest protruded in pride, a broad grin on his round face. His tiny tawny eyes mere slits with his joy.

Laila nodded. What more could she add to his unflinching faith and happiness?

A few months into his lessons, Manu was writing sentences and reading from children's picture books.

"I sign my name today, madam. For my salary." Manu's pride knew no bounds. "No X for Manu."

Laila glowed. Her student's pride was infectious.

"Thank you, my madam." He touched his heart. With palms joined together on his forehead, he walked backwards, leaving the apartment on cloud nine.

***

The sweltering Bahraini heat rose in a haze. The sea was a blurry, milky blue. Bobbing turtles swam in slow motion. Laila sat under the shade of the parasol, thinking back to her friendship with Malia. Why was jealousy the number one reason for the breakup of friendships?

Malia and Laila had been close, but Laila hadn't taken to her immediately like she had with Divya years ago in Saudi Arabia. The Gemini in her was conflicted about this new friendship—the duality of the twins, each side of her personality wanting its own way.

She'd met Malia at one of the many dinners that she and Kurt were invited to. Malia's husband was an ambassador, and she was a bored housewife looking to brush up her English. She was the epitome of a girl's girl. Tall and slender, boasting a shock of dark brown curls with a Julia Roberts mouth and doe eyes. She was the kind of woman who fluffed her hair ever so often, smoothed down her clothes and laughed delicately at the appropriate times. She wasn't the kind of woman who sported wedgies or chipped nail polish!

Laila admired women like Malia, who could effortlessly curl a strand of hair around their index finger or run all five fingers through it, apply lipstick without a mirror and look bashfully at men, batting their lashes prettily. Some women oozed sex appeal, turning men to putty in their hands. Laila wasn't one of them.

Voluptuous wasn't a word that could be used to describe Laila. Bodies squeezed into dresses two sizes smaller, smooth breasts bulging out of plunging necklines, and derrières that could balance a champagne glass a la Kim Kardashian were out of the question for her. She was small-breasted and slender, weighing less than fifty kilos at five feet two inches. She was far too prim to dare to bare! A prude. Her travels had taught her that men preferred women who were seen—busty and leggy—not heard. Someone beautiful on their arms to show off like a prized ornament. What happened, Laila wondered, to "Running the World" or being an "Independent Woman", as Beyoncé suggested in her songs?

Her friendship with Malia started with English conversation classes. She wanted lessons three times a week. Malia wasn't popular with the other mothers. They thought her too haughty. Some women just rubbed other women the wrong way.

Laila knew how it felt to be an outsider. She was sure it was more shyness than snobbishness.

The classes soon became a pretext. Malia hated speaking English, and the entire hour was spent gossiping in French about life in Manama. The best souks, spices, saris, and shisha!

With time, the conversation turned to mild gossip about the mothers in school. Their lack of style and badly brought-up children.

"Why do western women think that flip-flops are trendy?" Malia curled a strand of hair around her index finger. "I don't even wear these things at home! Did you see Martha's feet? Surely she can afford a pedicure."

"No I didn't! All I noticed were those ugly Crocs. They're even worse than the Birkenstock sandals that were trending a few years earlier!"

"Have you met the new Lebanese ambassador's wife? Fake nose, fake chin, fake lips, fake boobs."

"How do you know?"

"Don't be stupid, Laila, it's so obvious. The pout of her lips is so exaggerated."

Laila winked. "Guess her children don't look anything like her!"

They griped on the lack of fashionistas. Younger women attended black-tie affairs in short dresses, leaving nothing to the imagination, and heels they buckled in—or bejewelled Scholl sandals! Makeup was either OTT or not at all.

What had happened to the days when these events were longed for? A chance to buy a new outfit and go to the hairdresser? Where an invitation was handwritten in calligraphy and hand-delivered? Not an email sent to a mailing list of everyone who was anyone.

"If they don't want to dress up for themselves, have the respect to dress up for the rest of us who have to look at them! A full-length mirror should be a staple in every house."

"They should apologise to the mirror!" Laila chortled.

"Exactly! They need more than one mirror." Malia laughed. "Why don't they take care of themselves? With maids, drivers and cooks, they have more than enough time to pamper themselves!"

"There's no need to buy designer outfits, but for black-tie occasions or formal events, Chaine des

Rotisseurs evenings or gala balls, there's a dress code clearly marked on the invitation. It's courtesy, which many of them lack. They would never be allowed into a ballroom in Europe, yet they get away with it in the Middle East. Shouldn't they make an effort for their husbands? There should be a clause in the wedding contract—appearances matter, until death do you part."

"Unfortunately, not everyone is as particular about appearance and cleanliness, Laila."

Their conversations would have made excellent dialogue on a reality show.

Malia was a liberal mother. Her children were on first name terms with her and her husband. Maman or Mummy made her feel old! At eight years of age, her son Andreas was discussing sex and homosexuality. Laila was wary whenever he came over to play with Lili and Lalita.

As the friendship grew, Malia would be seen more and more at the hotel pool with her boys. Dinners at the embassy were now catered by the hotel. The executive chef went personally to cook at the residence, a privilege.

Sonya appeared on the scene. She was Russian, married to a wealthy Bahraini. She and Malia were two peas in a pod. Barbie dolls pouting and fidgeting with their hair. Sonya was as fragile as a freshly bloomed orchid. She had perfect blonde hair that fell in waves to her shoulders and peaches-and-cream skin. She floated. Stepping from one cloud to another, without disturbing the air around her. A tsarina. She spoke barely over a whisper. Everything about her was as delicate as a snowdrop.

Her husband's prosperity reflected in her immaculate dress sense. Her favourite designers were

Prada and Mui Mui. She had a range of handbags from common Vuitton—everyone who was anyone was toting one—to Dior and Gucci to Chanel and Hermes. Her favourite colour was fuchsia. Fuchsia outfits, fuchsia lipstick, fuchsia nail polish. Her cars went with her outfits, from a flaming red Porsche to a silver Maserati to a bilious Lamborghini to a burgundy Aston Martin and a fuchsia Mercedes coupe for the fuchsia days, which were often.

The changes in Malia were subtle in the beginning, like they'd been with Phyliss. Classes were cancelled in favour of coffees with Sonya. Play dates at the hotel pool were fewer. Shopping sprees and sales dates were postponed, then cancelled.

Was Laila jealous of Malia's friendship with Sonya?

She was as different from the two of them as a rose to a marigold, but Malia felt threatened. She ensured that Laila and Sonya's paths never crossed. Was she afraid Sonya would prefer Laila to her?

"Laila, is that you? It's Sonya." Her voice came down the phone as soft as a whisper. "I'd like to invite you to my house for tea on Wednesday at four p.m. Will you be able to make it?"

"Yes, I can, Sonya," Laila said carefully, surprised by the invitation. Wednesday was the start of the weekend in Bahrain—not very practical, with the girls finishing school at midday instead of 3:00 p.m.

She debated the wisdom of her decision. It was pure folly to accept, but curiosity got the better of her. Malia never missed an opportunity to gush about Sonya's palatial home. She wanted to see it for herself.

But the palace Laila had mentally prepared herself for turned out to be a quaint cottage on the outskirts of town. It was picture perfect. Sonya had cut-and-pasted a cottage from Norfolk, garden and all, to the Middle East, thatch roof included. It was an oasis in a desert city. The wallpaper in the sitting room was Laura Ashley florals, a real-life doll's house with tan leather armchairs and Victorian lampshades. Silver-framed photographs of the family were scattered on polished side tables and the mantelpiece over the roaring fireplace. The crackling wood drew a warm ambiance in December, a cool month in Bahrain.

"Welcome to my home, Laila. I'm so pleased you could come," Sonya said in her barely audible voice.

She brushed the air with two kisses and a whiff of Amouage. Laila smiled her thanks just as Malia made an entrance.

"Laila! What a surprise! I didn't expect to see you here," Malia said, flustered. She was clearly thrown off guard. It took her a moment to recover. The colour in her cheeks was a shade lighter than the scarlet tulips she held in her hand.

Sonya was oblivious to the undercurrent in her doll's house.

Laila tried to smooth out the tension in the room with talk of school homework and activities, but Malia was set on spoiling the afternoon with her jealousy.

"What did you major in, Laila?" she asked out of the blue.

"You know I didn't go to university, Malia," Laila answered quietly, having disclosed this information during one of the English lessons. Financial constraints in the Cardoso household hadn't allowed for higher education.

"Really? You didn't go to university. I've never met anyone who hasn't been to university."

"Really? Then you don't know many people."

Barbie-doll Sonya seemed to be in her own world. She couldn't care less what turmoil her invitation was causing.

Alternating between looking at her well-manicured nails or staring out at her English-style garden, she was lost in a reverie. Every few minutes, she would jingle a tiny silver bell in her left hand, and out of thin air, a butler would appear with more hot water or milk, wafer-thin cucumber and cream cheese sandwiches or scones. It reminded Laila of a scene from *Downton Abbey*.

The afternoon tea wasn't as pleasurable as Laila had anticipated. She felt uncomfortable and sad at the same time at Malia's insecurity.

Malia, on the other hand, sat with a smug look. She had won!

How could she call herself a friend? Laila wondered. Why was she so insecure? Laila made her excuses, unable to compete with Malia's barbs. She mentally made a note not to accept invitations from Sonya again.

She needn't have worried.

"Sonya is *my* friend. Please stay away."

Laila wasn't given a chance to reply before the dialling tone rang loud in her ear. It was less than half an hour since she had gotten back from Sonya's afternoon tea.

Laila considered calling Malia back but thought better of it. Sonya could be her exclusive property. Laila didn't lack for friends. She kept busy the way she had in Dubai, with decorating jobs. The Bahraini clients paid better than their Emirati counterparts.

Sonya called again a few weeks later for a ladies' lunch, but Laila politely declined the invitation.

Malia would feel threatened, and Laila didn't want that.

The English classes had come to an abrupt end, and Malia made sure to blank Laila out at the school gate.

Expats often took themselves too seriously, their superiority sticking out like a flashing red siren, warning people not of their level to keep their distance. Dealing with jealousy was easy. Racism not as much. She was used to the dismissive looks at functions. The limp handshake with no eye contact. The disinterest when she mentioned her name. Why bother with the Indian? What could she contribute to their high life? Surely, her husband would be a menial employee at any one of the shopping centres.

When Claudia invited Lili to play with her daughter Nicola, Laila accepted the invitation over the phone without hesitation. Shy Lili got along well with Nicola. As Laila still had to pick up Lalita, she'd met Claudia at the school, after the class teacher pointed her out.

"I'm Lili's mother. Thank you for inviting her over."

"You're not European?" Claudia was flabbergasted. She looked like she had seen an alien.

"I'm Kenyan Indian." Laila smiled pleasantly.

The familiar feeling of being less worthy was wearing Laila's patience thin. The expat community in the Middle East were extremely pretentious. Why was her skin colour a bone of contention? It was the twenty-first century, not the Middle Ages. She was better dressed, not in a drab cotton skirt and dirty white Crocs. Would it be easier if she dressed like Claudia?

"I didn't know. I thought you were French. You speak it very well. Without any accent."

"Is there a problem?" Laila wasn't going to let her intimidate her. Was Nicola only allowed to play with 'European' playmates?

"No! There's no problem, but I just remembered that Nicola has a dentist appointment. Can we do this another day?"

Laila was shocked. How dare she. There wasn't a twinge of remorse or embarrassment on Claudia's face. Lili had looked forward to the afternoon and was tearing up. Nicola retorted that she didn't have any appointments until next week.

"Nicola, *si c'est aujourd'hui*! We'll invite your friend another time." Claudia strode off, a reluctant Nicola in tow bawling her eyes out, still insisting that there was no dental appointment.

They had been dismissed.

The nerve. Laila wanted to throw something at Claudia's thick head. Instead, she took Lili in her arms and hugged her.

"Don't cry, my Lili."

"Why, Mama? Why did Nicola's mummy say she had to go to the dentist?"

How would she explain to her ten-year-old daughter that it was her mother's skin colour that had cost her the afternoon? There would be many Claudias in the future. Laila prayed her sensitive daughter would cope with such people with dignity and diplomacy, and not let these hurdles trip her.

What was wrong with human nature? Do we progress with technology to regress with humanity? Wouldn't there be less hatred and wars if we saw beyond a person's colour or creed?

Racists, Laila contemplated, were worse than assassins, pirates or murderers. There were only so many people they could hurt. Racists, on the other hand, targeted everyone. Their job description was wide and far-ranging.

When John Lennon sang "Imagine", did he really think that people could live as one?

CHAPTER 9

"MAN IN THE MIRROR"

February 2006

The nomadic lifestyle was taking a toll on Laila. Twenty years of being intrepid travellers from continent to continent was no longer as exciting as it had been.

Lili and Lalita had flown the nest. They were leading their lives in Europe, enjoying every moment of being young, independent adults.

Kurt was busy with work, and Laila was at a loose end. The crisis in their relationship had changed them from lovers to friends. However, she was happy. They talked about everything and anything-work, politics, people, places, friends, enemies, and sports. They never tired of sitting side by side in the evenings, talking. They would watch movies in the evenings Laila's head on Kurt's shoulder. There couldn't have been a more solid friendship, but it had taken Laila a long time to get back her confidence as a woman.

Any betrayal is devastating, but having to come to terms that the man you love wholly and deeply, someone you considered a soulmate, is attracted to the same sex is ground-shattering. Anger and hurt had gradually subsided to be replaced by love—not *in* love, just love. Time is a great healer, and Laila could honestly say she had finally healed.

Lili and Lalita couldn't have asked for a more loving father. They flourished under his constant guidance. If people talked, Laila never heard about it, or perhaps she wasn't listening. Laila thought of Kurt and her as two individuals who shared a heart. They were a happy family.

But Laila needed to do more with her life. She had time to spare with the girls no longer around. Laila's fingers were itching to help the less fortunate. The world was a difficult place to live in; her experience in Congo taught her that.

How she laughed when Lakshmi said time flies. She'd been in her twenties and invincible. There was nothing she couldn't do or be. It didn't seem so funny anymore. Time had slipped by in a flash, quick as a tyre change at the Grand Prix. Did time go by faster with age?

The nineties were wonderful years. There were days when they seemed a lifetime ago, and other days they seemed like yesterday. Twenty years later, things had changed, and not necessarily for the better.

Laila could feel herself getting old. Her once high cheekbones were sagging minutely every day. The crease between her eyebrows was getting deeper; the crow's feet around her eyes looked more like nests. She made a conscious effort to not to look in the mirror until she had washed her face. It was far too depressing to deal with the signs of ageing in the morning.

The days when she would look at her reflection in every mirror, car or shop window were long gone.

How vain she had been. Now, she avoided mirrors at all costs.

Sometimes she considered Botox injections or fillers to help the ageing process but then thought better of it. She wasn't going for the artificial look. The lines told their own story. She didn't want to be in the same bracket as flimsy women whose looks mattered above all, who only took photos and selfies from a certain angle. No angle could make a person have a good or kind heart, be compassionate or humble, even intelligent.

Dealing with menopausal hot flushes was like a match being struck at the tip of her toes to spark an inferno rising rapidly to the top of her head. Beads of sweat covering every inch of her body. The embarrassment in public making it worse! When was the last time she'd had a good night's sleep? The night sweats were uncomfortable, drenching her for long minutes, then leaving her cold, clammy and exhausted. The constant padding to the bathroom to wipe her body down.

Life changes together with hormonal changes weren't boding well. Her weight, which had been a constant, was deserting her. The kilos seemed to pile up overnight. Tennis, golf and aerobics weren't budging the flab. The less she ate, the more she weighed! It was a vicious cycle.

If only there was a fountain of youth.

If Laila didn't realise that life was short, the news of popular singers dying brought that to the forefront. Prince, whom she had adored while growing up. "Purple Rain", "Time", "Diamonds and Pearls"—Laila knew every hit of his off the top of her head. Whitney Houston's "I Will Always Love

You". Michael Jackson's "Black or White" or George Michael's "Careless Whisper".

Laila had always loved music from Bob Marley, UB40, Bucks Fizz, Coldplay, David Bowie and Queen to Eminem, P!nk, Ed Sheeran, Adele, Elvis Presley and Leanne Rimes. The boring old songs of the fifties and sixties that Lakshmi used to listen to and she would roll her eyes at were now her favourites. Dean Martin, Frank Sinatra, Frankie Valli, Bing Crosby, Edith Piaf, Ray Charles were golden oldies. Laila remembered how she and Tamer had never missed one *Solid Gold* episode on Sundays in the eighties. They'd wait impatiently for 9:00 p.m. in front of the black and white telly, fascinated by the dancers in their lame sequined outfits.

She missed how television used to be. *The Fresh Prince of Bel-Air, Mork and Mindy, The Jeffersons* and *Family Matters*, light-hearted comedies, not the violent police series or reality shows produced today. Skimpy clothes, sex, violence, hatred, drugs, alcohol and bad language attracted the new generation.

She missed the carefree days of Pearl and Dean movies at the drive-in, a monthly treat that Laila had looked forward to.

"Are we going to the drive-in tonight, Ma?" she'd ask Lakshmi.

"Yes, my child. Do your homework when you get home from school. We'll go for the seven-thirty p.m. show."

The picnic basket would be packed with sausages, fried beef cutlets in soft buns, chips with mayonnaise and tomato ketchup and queen cakes. She and Tamer had their own speaker hanging from the car window, cosy under the blanket.

It had all been replaced by Netflix, unlimited movies in the comfort of your home.

Was Laila getting too old? What happened to the art of writing a letter on crisp paper with a fountain pen? Facebook, Twitter, Instagram—all the various social media available—were Greek to Laila. Why would anyone want to display their private lives to the world? Why would you post photos of the food you ate? Were your friends even interested in what was eaten and where or with whom? Did anyone care about holiday photos of swaying palms and margaritas while they were behind a desk trying to complete a report that was needed two days ago?

What happened to the days when a photograph was considered an outing? Where best clothes were worn with a beaming smile in place, anxiously awaiting the flash of the camera?

She had to move with the flow, but Laila found it difficult. She couldn't make technology her friend. It had its perks, like talking to Lili and Lalita almost every day, Laila had to admit that!

***

The apartment in the hotel was bright and sunny. Full-length windows gave panoramic views of the Atlantic Ocean. Spectacular Mopane trees dotted the verdant garden, large branches giving ample shade for guests eating breakfast al fresco.

Karina was Laila's friend, whose laughter filled a room with sparkles, the kind lit on birthday cakes. She was always happy. Her emerald eyes would twinkle with merriment and her small mouth would break into a ready smile come rain or sun.

Nisha, Karina's daughter, was in the same class as Lili, so the friendship grew from a few words outside the school gate to lunches, and dinners, and afternoons spent by the pool with the girls splashing and frolicking in the sun.

Karina's husband ran a thriving business; money posed no problem for her. Unlike the nouveau riche, Karina was subtle with her wealth. Jewellery and designer wear were never overstated or loud. Brand names were never emblazoned on clothing, handbags, shoes or jewellery. She never wore makeup; she didn't need it with her flawless complexion. She was gracious, kind, generous, intelligent, bubbly and witty. Laila felt comfortable with Karina, like she had felt with Narmin and Julia. They were close.

Then, Laila got a phone call.

"I need to see you desperately," Karina said.

"I'm just finishing a game of tennis."

"I'll be there in five minutes."

Karina hung up.

Laila sensed something afoot. Karina was usually poised, but today she sounded flustered. It was unlike her friend. What could have happened so early in the morning?

At the restaurant, Karina gave Laila the customary two kisses on both cheeks. She looked forlorn. A deep frown creased her tiny forehead, making her look older than her thirty-eight years. Her makeup-free face was flushed like she had climbed a hill.

"I have to talk to you. It's killing me."

"Okay, I'm listening. Tea?"

"I couldn't swallow anything. I've fallen in love." Karina dropped her statement in one breath. Turning scarlet.

"What? What do you mean, fallen in love?"

"I'm in love. What am I going to do, Laila? You've got to help me. The chemistry is shocking between us." Karina's sentences came out in short spurts.

"Slow down, Karin. You can't just fall in love," Laila said, beckoning a waiter.

Karina was a bomb ready to explode. Tea would have to do, and it was too early to hit the bottle, even though both of them rarely drank. Their conversation would be private. English was hardly spoken; the Angolese were proud Portuguese speakers.

"He's a married man. We met at a party several weeks ago. Our eyes met across the room. I know you think this is out of a Mills and Boon, but it isn't. I've never felt like this. Tahir was my first love. We married after high school. The chemistry was never like this with Tahir. I've been meeting Imran like a teenager at odd places, but it's getting difficult. Yesterday we met at the supermarket! The touch of his hand on mine makes me break out in goosebumps! I've been skipping on cloud nine."

The words spilled out of Karina's mouth, gushing like a broken dam. Sentence after sentence, each one making Laila re-live her own experience with Kurt, albeit a different kind.

"Slow down. Next, you'll be telling me that you hear violins." Laila made light of the situation, but Karina's secret had ripped open her own wound, which had healed over the years but was still tender. Laila would always be in love with Kurt.

"We kissed yesterday. What a kiss, Laila. My knees buckle thinking of it. I was in heaven, with tingling sensations running up and down my spine. The way he held my face in his hands. The slow movement of his lips against mine. It was heavenly, Laila. I think of him all the time, every waking minute. It was only a kiss, Laila; nothing else, I promise. You believe me, don't you?"

"I don't care what it was. He's *married*, for God's sake, Karina." It came out harshly. "You know he's not going to leave his wife for you. They never do."

The image of Kurt kissing the PA of the Royal Diwan was clearly etched before her eyes. She was reliving the moment again, in slow motion. Laila blinked, but the image remained.

"Whose side are you on? Please, Laila." Karina paused, holding her head in her hands. "You're probably right. The guilt is killing me. Last night I couldn't even let Tahir kiss me good night. Tahir works seven days a week; the company is *his* first love."

Laila prised Karina's slim fingers from her face, squeezing them.

"I can't remember the last time we really talked," Karina said. "He's more out of the country than in. Our relationship isn't what it was. We never do things together. I spend all my time with the children. I attend school meetings, events, tennis competitions and piano recitals by myself. I don't remember when we last made love." She threw up her hands in frustration, then brushed away her angry tears with the back of her hands.

"I'm so sorry, Karina. Why didn't you tell me?"

"Because I didn't mind. I bobbed along the waves of day-to-day life. It didn't matter. Now it does. I feel wanted. Special. It makes a big difference. I even feel beautiful instead of ordinary."

"Are you crazy? Ordinary is not a word I would use on you, Karina. Extraordinary is more like it."

With her curly hair, eyelashes like a giraffe, dense and thick, and green eyes, Karina looked like an exotic Disney character.

"What am I going to do? I feel like I'm betraying Tahir. I've never lacked for anything nor have the children. He's an impeccable provider. We go on vacations a couple of times a year, buy the best clothes and eat in the best Michelin star restaurants. I have two maids, a driver and a chef. What more could I ask for?"

Expatriate life was not as wonderful as many thought. A big paycheque at the end of the month couldn't make up for lonely hours or lack of affection and attention.

Laila didn't know how to answer Karina. Silence stretched.

"I'm so confused," Karina said. "All I know is that I really enjoy these snatched minutes with Imran. I don't know if I want the stolen kisses to stop or for things to go further. I'm sure last night Tahir could hear my pounding heart." Tears slid down her rosy cheeks. "Tahir is an invisible father and husband. I don't know what to do, Laila. Should I tell him?" Karina finally asked.

"No! Don't do that." Laila had to restrain herself from shouting the words. "It was only a kiss. As long as it remains just a kiss, there's no need to spill the beans to Tahir. It will only upset him. Do you want to put your kids through this turmoil? Cool down, Karina."

Laila knew that one day she would have to come clean with Lili and Lalita about Kurt. It would be a difficult conversation. Perhaps the hardest one she'd ever have.

"I should tell Tahir. The guilt is killing me."

"Better it kills you than Tahir. It was only a kiss." Laila tried to play the devil's advocate. "Listen to me, you can't tell him."

"No, Laila. I have to come clean. I'll break it off with Imran. It's for the best."

"Okay, break it off with Imran. But why tell Tahir? Think of his reaction. Let it be, Karin. Please." Laila looked pleadingly at her friend. She knew intuitively that Tahir wouldn't react graciously.

Karina was lost in a world of her own. She barely seemed to listen to what Laila had to say. Abruptly, she stood. She picked up her leather tote bag that was draped over the bamboo pool chair.

"I have to go, Laila."

Laila tried to grab Karina's slender arm, but she brushed past, practically running to the car park. "Don't do something you'll regret, Karin. Think for just one minute." Laila ran after her friend.

"No, Laila. I've been stupid. No matter how Imran makes me feel, I'm a married woman and I can't behave like this. I'll call you."

She slammed the door of the silver Audi shut and revved the engine.

Laila stared after the speeding car, baffled at how quickly the conversation had ended.

She spent the rest of the morning pacing the floor of the apartment, anxiously waiting for the phone to ring.

Tahir was a good guy, intelligent, kind and extremely knowledgeable about technology. He was a tall, well-built man with glasses that constantly slipped off his nose, a nose he was permanently blowing due to allergies. He was an excellent provider for his family financially, but money—however much one has of it—can't buy happiness, Laila thought distractedly.

At lunchtime, Laila jumped into the car. She would have an opportunity to see Karina at school.

But instead, the maid was standing outside the gate. Alarm bells went clanking off. It had to be a grave matter for Karina not to pick up her daughters from school. She and Laila were the only two mothers who were there religiously. They wouldn't pan their children off on the maid.

"*Senhora?*" Laila asked Karina's maid.

"*Ela tem uma dor de cabeca.*" She has a headache.

Laila debated whether to call Karina or to wait. No news is good news, or so she thought. Finally, after lunch, the suspense was too much to bear.

"I can't talk," Karina said. "I'll meet you tomorrow at nine at the hotel car park."

The phone clicked.

The next day, Karina was waiting as agreed in the car park, her eyes red and swollen. Her cheeks were puffy, and her normally perfect hair was a dishevelled mess. She wore the same clothes as the day before. She looked like she had just come out of the tumble dryer.

"What's the matter, Karin?" Laila took her friend's hands in hers. They were icy.

Karina burst into tears. She dabbed at her nose with a torn, shredded tissue. Laila thrust a packet into her hand from her handbag.

"I told Tahir."

"Oh, Lord. Why?" Laila wanted to shake her friend to her senses.

"I'm not to see you. I've just managed to get rid of the driver."

"Me? What have I done?"

"Tahir says you're a bad influence on me." Karina looked so desolate, it broke Laila's heart.

"How did he come to that conclusion?"

"He says, as you're non-Muslim, you wouldn't know how relationships work."

Laila wanted to scream. The sniffling man who was never present for his family knew. Non-Muslims didn't fall in love? Didn't they have feelings?

"I realise that I made a mistake, Laila. I should have listened to you." Laila had to bite her tongue to stop the *I told you so!* "I was better off living with the guilt. He was livid. He ranted on that I've slept with Imran. He called me a whore and a liar. Said I've disgraced his name in the community. It was unbearable, the insults he hurled at me, Laila."

"I'm so sorry, Karin."

How could she assuage her friend's pain? Sorry? A small word that didn't dive into the complexities of the pain and injustice her friend was going through.

Laila took Karina's hands and held them.

"He wanted to know details of where we had met, how long has it been going on, and is the sex better. He reacted so badly that I didn't dare mention the kiss. He's convinced that I had sex with Imran. I'm worse off than before. I can't stop thinking what a stupid mistake I've made. I can't stop crying."

"Crying won't get you anywhere. Pull yourself together. Once he calms down, it will get better. Give him time. You both need time." She sounded like Lakshmi, Laila realised.

"There's more to tell. He wants me to go to the imam to confess my sins, as he calls them. He says it's the only way he can forgive me. How can I go to the imam? The entire community will know. Nothing could be more embarrassing than that!"

"Tahir's way of dealing with the problem is to pick up a stone? My poor Karin." Laila hugged her friend while the tears fell. "How can I help? Tell me.

He doesn't want you to see me. Why? Men need someone to blame; it's never their fault."

"He's left instructions with the maid that you shouldn't be allowed to enter the house. He's even taken away my phone. We're meant to go to the mosque together this evening so I can confess to the imam in front of him."

"Has he lost it? How far will he take this? He wants his pound of flesh. A pound today, a kilo tomorrow."

"I've hurt his ego. I was wrong; it's payback time."

"Don't be stupid, Karin. Stop blaming yourself."

"I have to leave. I'll be a prisoner in my own home. I'll call you whenever I can." Karina squeezed Laila's hand for a long moment. "Think of me. Say a prayer for me." Green eyes swam in tears.

Laila swallowed the giant lump in her throat. What a mess. Karina would pay a high price for a few stolen moments of bliss.

***

A few days later, Laila got a hasty call. The Imam had told Karina that to repent, she was to pray five times a day like a good Muslim. She had to help him with religious classes for children on a daily basis.

"He's forbidden me to see or speak to Imran. I have to be the humble, meek, submissive Muslim wife. To be at his beck and call." Karina cried softly.

"What? Why?"

"There's more. You're not the type of friend I should be keeping company with. I have to relegate you to the recycle bin," Karina said, trying to put some humour.

"What?" Laila was livid.

"You're not a worthy friend. I should find religious friends, women who'll give me good advice on caring for my husband and children. I have to gain the seat at Allah's right hand."

Karin explained that with these women, she would read the Koran and pray. This was the only way she could redeem herself.

Laila's blood was bubbling. "What happened to the God of love and forgiveness? This is incredible, Karin."

Karina's sobbing over the phone broke Laila's heart. She could hear the misery in her voice. Karina was never a religious person; the punishment would be onerous.

The dial tone sounded in Laila's ear. Someone had entered the room.

***

Weeks went by without Laila seeing her friend. At school, the maid picked up and dropped off Nisha and Soraya.

There was no way of reaching Karina. The phone was off.

Laila dared to slip a note with the maid begging Karina to meet her.

A few days later, she got a reply. Karina missed the outside world and their times together. Her life revolved around the mosque, religious classes and praying. The women who claimed to be her friends found fault with all she did. Tahir barely spoke to her. He said he had forgiven her but would never trust her again. She was lonelier than before, and if it wasn't for her children, she didn't think she could continue with life.

Laila cried for her friend. She understood how she felt. She had been there as a victim. Circumstances were different, but heartbreak was the same.

Some months later Laila met Karina at a cocktail party. Tahir nodded coldly in her direction but spoke to Kurt like he was his long-lost friend. Laila's once bubbly friend had been replaced by a serious woman who wore her smile on her lips but not in her eyes. Her beautiful hair was covered by a veil. The long black skirt looked ridiculous, the shapeless blouse even worse! Karina resembled a flimsy paper bag. She looked like a gazelle trapped in the headlights of a car.

"You okay?" Laila hugged her bony frame.

"I'll live," Karina said hollowly. She squeezed Laila's hand. "I miss you so much." She brushed a wayward tear with the back of her hand, casting a furtive glance in Tahir's direction.

"Can't we meet, even for a short while? I miss you too. Look at you! You're not the Karin I know."

"He won't let me. I've begged and pleaded." She couldn't talk as emotion engulfed her. She shook her head slightly. "I'm fine. Really. It isn't as bad as it looks."

"He's such an ass. And you're *not* fine. Are you eating? You're being punished for having a friend who doesn't brainwash you with religious nonsense. It's absurd. I'll talk to Tahir." Laila was fuming, an angry dragon spewing fire.

"No! It will make matters worse. I've accepted it. I should have listened to you. It's too late." Laila's heart cried for her friend. "I'm fine. Summer is approaching; I'll be going back to Istanbul with the kids for a few weeks. It will do us good, the change."

Tahir was suddenly by his wife's side. He held Karina by the elbow, escorting her away. She turned briefly, gave Laila a lopsided smile and a tiny wave. She put on a brave face.

That was the last time Laila saw Karina. A few notes were exchanged before she left for the summer. Calls went unanswered. Laila went by the house one afternoon, but the askari staunchly refused to open the gate to her. Even a bribe of dollars—Angolese kwanza—wouldn't work.

After summer, Kurt was posted to Yemen, and they were on the move again.

The sun had set, turning the sky peachy orange and purple. It was beautiful. Serene. How long had she been lost in her reverie? It was years since they were in Angola. She hoped Karina had found the happiness she deserved. That laughter had returned to burst out of her friend.

***

September 2007

Kurt was in Singapore for a seminar, and the week stretched before Laila. She was curled on the cream leather sofa, novel facedown. It wasn't as riveting as the blurb made out.

She closed her eyes and immediately was in Malawi. She could hear the rhythm of the falling rain, actually smell the mustiness in the air. The wet red earth was comforting. The elephant ear shrubs glistened with water droplets, washed clean of red dust in the downpour. The trees and hedges shone. The rains were welcome after the long dry spell. The vivid image brought a smile to Laila's lips.

Malawi was a poor country; the sea of plastic bottles floating in the gutters after each downpour was an eyesore. Streets were open markets where vendors sold everything from food items to broomsticks, clothes, phones and sunglasses. Almost anything could be found. Mothers with tiny babies on their backs peddled wares for a few coins.

Laila's mind wandered down memory lane, stopping at Zubeida. She winced, remembering her unpleasant experience.

Warning bells had rung out to keep a distance when they were introduced, but Laila had ignored her intuition. If ever there was a woman who didn't listen to her God-given gift, it was Laila. Instead of reading the signs, Laila embraced the friendship wholeheartedly. Zubeida was the first person she had met on her arrival in Malawi. A friend in a new country helps you to learn the ropes, or so naïve Laila thought.

Zubeida was the wife of the director of engineering at the hotel. She had arrived in Malawi thirty years ago from Lebanon. An initial contract of two years had out-run its time. Her husband Rojan had risen through the ranks and was approaching sixty—and Kurt had been instructed by the head office to ensure that Rojan took his retirement.

Zubeida's petty jealousy of Laila's youth and lifestyle had been a thorn in her side, but after Kurt's declaration of Rojan's retirement by the end of the year, it became a full-blown spear! Festering like gangrene.

Laila's arrival had usurped Zubeida's long-standing position in the country. The last few general managers had been single. For Zubeida, Kurt's wife and children upset her equation at the most sort after five-star hotel in the country. A young thirty-odd-year-old was too bitter a pill to swallow. Her world as she knew it was changing.

"Meet Laila, the wife of the general manager of the hotel. She's young, but she'll learn," was Zubeida's standard introduction of Laila at functions.

Was that a threat? Was Laila's age in question? What was she going to learn?

Laila always mentally rolled her eyes, choosing to ignore Zubeida's comments. She pitied her, trying so hard to hold on to her youth in her dress sense, false lashes, plastic nose and breasts, coloured contact lenses and mannerisms. Laila laughed off all Zubeida's persistent attempts to get her to change her dress sense, her hairstyle and sporty side.

"You should let your hair grow; it's far too short. It's boyish."

It's my look and I like it, Laila thought.

"Accessorize more. Chunky jewellery is in fashion."

Chunky jewellery would have swallowed up Laila's stature.

"Why hasn't Kurt bought you a Rolex? People here need to see that you can afford such things."

Zubeida always sported her own gold Rolex, her mark of impression. But a watch didn't necessarily mean she'd have time for the important things in life.

"A diamond ring should be three carats or more, otherwise it's not worth buying. They are mined here; you can get a good-sized uncut stone for a decent price."

Where would Laila find someone to cut the stone for her? De Beers wouldn't come knocking on Laila's apartment door looking for her. Were they meant to do the job at a throwaway price because of her name?

"You should put on more weight. People will think your husband doesn't feed you."

You would like me to look more like you, on the heavier side.

"Why do you order the nanny a meal in the evenings? She'll be happy to eat your daughters' leftovers. Surely they don't eat a whole portion."

How can you even think like that?

"You shouldn't greet the staff whenever you pass them. You're the wife of the boss. Ignore them."

Is that how you were brought up?

"The wine you served last night tasted like camembert soaked in vinegar."

You must drink Camembert soaked in vinegar often to recognise the taste!

"I love being driven around in the Mercedes; it gets me from A to B in style."

You can also get from A to B on a bicycle!"

Zubeida craved the limelight. Nothing happened without her knowing. She needed to be the belle of the ball, openly canvassing for invitations. It upset her when invitations she'd received for years were redirected to Mr and Mrs K. Petticoat. She was being relegated to second position.

After so many years in the country, the future was foggy for Zubeida and Rojan. It was hard for Zubeida to envision the future outside of Africa. The life and perks were good in comparison to what awaited them.

Accusing fingers were pointed at Kurt. He wanted to get rid of them; he didn't know what he was doing. He was getting too big for his boots. Rojan was an asset for the hotel; why get rid of an asset?

She would openly ignore Laila at functions or in the hotel lobby. It gave her great pleasure to snub Laila in public. She was the doyenne in Malawi. No one was going to replace her.

Laila wondered why she had become Zubeida's target. The discontent was between them, Kurt and the organisation. Age, of course, doesn't spring out like a jack-in-the-box—Rojan's retirement shouldn't have come as a surprise.

Expatriate communities thrive on gossip, and soon tongues started wagging.

"How come Zubeida walked past you at the function yesterday?" Aurelia, the wife of the Canadian high commissioner, asked. "I thought you got along well with her."

Laila shrugged her slim shoulders. "Did she? I didn't notice."

"She's telling everyone that Kurt is heartless. That he's sacking Rojan after years of dedicated service."

It was a wonder Zubeida hadn't grown a nose like Pinocchio.

"Sacking him? Really?" Laila raised a perfect eyebrow. "Everyone has to retire at some point. Sixty is retirement age in the hotel industry. Rojan knows that."

"Well, she told me in confidence that 'management' is getting rid of him. She's really upset and was crying."

The Academy Award goes to Zubeida for best actress! When does the acting stop and reality kick in?

"Excuse me, Alexandra is calling." Laila waved to an imaginary person in the crowd.

Zubeida had the gift of gab and knew how to use it to her advantage. Laila's personality and discreet ways were chicken feed for a woman like her. The rumours she spread infuriated Laila, who wanted to confront her, but Kurt wanted no part in it and insisted that Laila let it go.

"Do you need to stoop to her level? Rojan hasn't said a word. She's the one stirring up trouble. She wants to see how far she can push you." Kurt paced up and down the bedroom. He never dabbled in gossip, preferring to concentrate on his work.

Laila wished she could ignore the situation, but it needled her.

Things got worse as Zubeida made a beeline for tennis and golf lessons. She started taking driving lessons and horse-riding classes, after thirty years with no interest in any of these activities.

Laila would bump into her on the tennis court or golf course. Zubeida blanked her out. It was awkward when the pro would look at them questioningly, knowing that they knew each other.

The month before Zubeida's departure was filled with farewell events. Laila and Kurt were excluded from all invitations. Tongues started wagging yet again. Kurt ignored them, Laila fumed! Zubeida was showing her true age, six instead of sixty! If she thought that omitting them from the guest list would hurt, she was sadly mistaken. They didn't lack for invitations to other events.

Dues had to be paid, and Rojan opted to have his retirement in a lump sum. It was no secret that they were looking to purchase a house in Beirut.

Kurt heard through the grapevine that Rojan was also negotiating for the same amount from the owner of the hotel.

"Rojan, I've checked with corporate. It seems that you can either be paid by the hotel or the owning company. Not by both," Kurt said, as kindly as possible.

"Really? I didn't know." Rojan flushed red.

"So, the cheque will come from the hotel?"

"Yes, of course," Rojan mumbled, avoiding eye contact with Kurt.

If things had been bad before, now they avalanched out of control.

Rojan was sullen, but Zubeida turned into a two-headed dragon. Snide remarks were directed at Laila.

Laila threw up her hands in disgust. "Why am I being targeted?"

Kurt shrugged. Who retired and when wasn't her decision to make, but any company decision seemed to be his wife's fault.

Zubeida spoke to whoever would listen, including junior staff. The sensible people ignored her rantings; others, of course, confronted Laila, rubbing their hands in glee in anticipation of juicy gossip.

Laila couldn't have been more dignified. She smiled, showed surprise, then walked away.

"Let me be the bigger person," Laila said. "I'm going to say goodbye to Rojan and Zubeida."

They would be leaving that evening for Lebanon.

"Are you sure, Laila, after all her nastiness recently?" Kurt looked at Laila worriedly.

Laila rang the doorbell cautiously, wondering at the wisdom of her decision. Zubeida opened the door and stared stone-faced at her.

"What do you want?" Her red lipstick was bleeding. She looked terrible. Laila felt sorry for her.

"I've come to say goodbye."

"Don't say another word. Rojan and I don't want your wishes. You're a nasty, horrible, evil person. We want nothing to do with the likes of you." Zubeida had turned the colour of her lipstick.

"What have I done, Zubeida?"

"Don't pretend not to know. You're the reason we have to leave. It's because of you that Rojan didn't get paid his fair share." She wagged her chipped-nail-polished finger inches from Laila's face.

Laila shuddered. "What are you talking about? I don't know why you're upset with me?" Anger was rising to the surface like yeast bubbles in warm milk. She held her hands together, resisting the urge to strike Zubeida.

"Bitches like you won't go far. How can you pretend not to know?" Zubeida prodded Laila's arm sharply.

"Zuzu, stop it now. Leave it alone." Rojan stood, looking apologetically at Laila. His shoulders were stooped, and he looked old and tired. "You better leave, Laila. It would be for the best."

"I don't deserve this, Rojan. What is Zubeida referring to?"

Why was she pleading for answers? Nothing would change Zubeida's convictions.

"Not guilty?" Zubeida screamed. "God knows what you told Kurt for him to throw us out of the hotel. To make us destitute."

Destitute? Laila wondered. With over a quarter-million dollars? Instead, she said, "Rojan has reached retirement age. Kurt is following the rules and—"

"Rules can be bent. It's your wickedness that's left us in this situation," Zubeida spat.

"My wickedness? I'm not making the rules here. How can you even think that? Not all rules can be bent." Laila sighed in utter frustration. "I wish you both well. Really I do."

Rojan, as per norm, stood silently beside his wife. Laila was sure it was Zubeida pulling all the strings, and Rojan the marionette followed in jerky movements.

"We don't need your wishes. Get lost."

Laila jumped at the vigour of the slamming door. She stared at it dumbly for several seconds. Angry tears fell. She wanted to ram down the door in frustration.

The sane side of her won. She shook her head and headed back to the apartment. It wasn't worth it. She wouldn't let the likes of Zubeida mar her stay in a country she had come to love.

Lakshmi had said to her many years ago, "Choose not friends from outer shores, for feathers float but pearls like below."

Daydreaming wasn't constructive, Laila thought, as she wiped her eyes. Zubeida had hurt her tremendously with her cruel words. Why did she cross paths with jealous women? She was rarely prone to jealousy. There was nothing wrong with envying people at the top of the ladder, but glance down every now and then to see how many more were at the bottom.

Laila was no longer the starry-eyed young girl who had left Nairobi years ago. She realised that in the expatriate world things worked differently. Competition, rivalry and jealousy were part of this rather bizarre community.

Perhaps in the suburbs of London, New York or Bangalore people were too busy with day-to-day living to worry about titles and positions. What their neighbours wore or how much they earned. How successful their children were and what car they drove. Who attended more receptions? Who rubbed shoulders with whom? It was petty and foolish, but then, they didn't have much else to do to while away the time in a foreign land!

CHAPTER 10

"CHOP"

May 2013

Laila stared at Kurt, not believing her ears. Another change. After all the hard work he had put into opening the hotel in Lagos. It was nothing short of a feat. The previous general manager had accomplished little in four years. He had lived the high life the Nigerian way, with the movers and shakers.

In a year, Kurt had managed to open the hotel. He worked fifteen hours a day, seven days a week. Often, she thought he was headed for a heart attack—or worse, a nervous breakdown. He was torn between the owner and bosses from head office. Staff were always paid late, while the wife of the owner paraded in the hotel lobby in Chanel, Dior and Gucci, oblivious to the hardship of the local people, who had school fees and rents to be paid besides everyday expenditure.

What happened to appreciation? Loyalty? A firm handshake? It seemed that colleagues' and bosses' only aim in the twenty-first century was to get to the top of the ladder regardless of the means. Blue-eyed boys—that didn't include Kurt—secured promotions after the hard work was done. They rode on the back of someone else. The ground-breaker discarded as easily as dusting flour off hands.

Were other conglomerations as cutthroat? Was Laila naïve in thinking that fair play mattered? *Walk the talk* didn't exist. Was there any point to the seminars and conferences? Practising the preaching was forgotten once the course ended! The corporate world gave kudos to colleagues with little integrity. Like a cult, they cajoled and pampered their own kind. Many would willingly kill to propel their careers.

"You have to be kidding me, Kurt," Laila said tiredly. "Why is there preferential treatment for some in your organisation?"

Kurt's career had revolved around hardship locations, barring a few exceptions in the Middle East. When no one in the organisation wanted a destination, it was offered to him. Was it because he never questioned the decision of corporate biggies or demanded better? Should he have been more forceful? Kurt didn't have nine lives like some of his colleagues.

"Have you pointed out how profits have rocketed since you took over from your predecessor? What about flagging results that have picked up by one hundred percent?" Laila was exasperated. "What about the well-deserved promotion?"

Business, like politics, is a dirty game. One had to be tough to get to the top. There was no room for kindness, honesty, compassion nor sensitivity, as in Kurt's case. It starts with soiled hands and escalates to soiled souls. If the line wasn't drawn, it was a zip-line to the other side. No godfather, as in Kurt's case, meant free-falling.

Kurt wasn't the kind of man who fired staff on the spur of the moment or told them off in public. He wasn't afraid to work with them, serving guests or making a bed when need be. He took time to explain things to them in detail. He fought tirelessly for salary increments and better working conditions, staff housing a priority. He wasn't the boss who thought only of his career path and how quickly he could climb the ladder. He never played politics, even though he knew this would lead to promotion. With Kurt at the helm, it was never dog eat dog. He was fair and kind. He was straighter than a coconut tree, work-wise!

If he had shone the right people's shoes, perhaps he would have been rewarded with the longed-for promotion. Kurt wasn't a shoe-shiner; he didn't know how to polish and buff. His tongue wasn't as smooth as Tennessee whisky. But when they'd left Egypt for Dubai, the staff had lined the lobby of the hotel to the entrance gate in single file to bid him farewell. The applause was tremendous.

"Your husband is too soft; he should have fired the front office manager for his oversight on the booking." Betty, the wife of the Resident Manager started the conversation while they sat drinking tea after the game of tennis.

Comments such as these always annoyed Laila.

"Well, if he was tougher, I think your husband would have been fired a long time ago!" Today Laila was not going to put up with such comments. Kurt's kindness was *not* a weakness.

Betty stared, gobsmacked.

Laila should have clapped her hands and danced a jig in joy. Leaving dirty, congested and unsafe Lagos after two years should have been welcome.

The filth and danger had been overwhelming in the beginning. Her cleanliness obsession had run amok. She was back to having sanitisers in every room, in all her handbags and in the car.

Funny how her time in the Congo had brought her OCD under control.

The Kalashnikov-wielding bodyguard who sat in the front seat of the white Pajero was a stress she could do without. He would turn every few minutes to openly gawp at her. Laila couldn't decide what was worse, the ogling or the loaded rifle?

She longed for the good old days of the abaya!

Constant traffic jams on Falomo Bridge to Victoria Island, humidity and tropical thunderstorms she could get used to, but gutters overflowing with discarded plastic sachets and bottles, papers, cartons, tins and faeces was a sight she would have preferred not to see. Bare butts lined the open drainage three times a day, a 3D view from the hotel's prestigious bay window. Medicinal, a way of hardening the skin of businessmen and newcomers.

Nigerians lived ostentatious lives. A competition of who could afford luxuries. Labels were left on sleeves of Boss, YSL or Dior suits. There was never a shortage of Hermes and Chanel handbags. Preachers had their own private jets. Piaget, Patek Philippe and Vacheron Constantin watches adorned the wrists of top-notch bosses—with or without diamonds, depending on the under-the-table packages.

Rolls Royce Phantoms were washed with Moet and Chandon Champagne. Those with money to spare used Magnum Rose! Maids from Thailand and Indonesia were a common sight. Proof that a local maid didn't require a work permit.

In Saudi Arabia, the UAE or Oman, wealth had abounded, but the wealthy were low profile and rarely flaunted their riches. In the Middle East, men and women had a uniform of gallabiyahs and abayas! There was no distinguishing a sheikh from a store-owner or street-sweeper.

Laila couldn't even dream of entering the league of rich. She would be disqualified before entry. Competing with younger women who looked down plastic noses at her love-handles and bingo wings was daunting. Botox treatment, tummy tuck, plastic surgery, breast enhancement or liposuction was for the rich and famous, or almost famous. She was battling with night sweats and hot flushes. Plucking grey pubic and eyebrow hairs was a hobby. Like Picasso wielding a paintbrush, she dyed hair roots every three weeks. That's how good Laila had become.

Wealth was vulgar and loud in Nigeria. Expats tried to blend in with wealthy locals sporting over the top designer wear, cars and positions, but competition was stiff. Name-dropping at every occasion was a sport. Red carpet affairs abounded. Would the president, the governor, CEOs of oil refineries, top-notch executives in billion-dollar-profit companies, and Nollywood stars be on the guest list? Invitations consisted of three or four cocktail parties in one evening, a dinner or cigars and a cognac after-party. Careful consideration of which function to be seen at had to be taken into account. Non-attendance would mean being struck off an invitation list. It was a whirlwind of social gatherings every day of the week.

It had been thrilling, in its way, and now it was being snatched away from her.

"Where to this time, Kurt?"

"They've offered Lusaka."

"You mean take it or leave."

"I need the job, Laila. There are university fees and the mortgage to be paid. I still have a few years to retirement. At my age, no one will employ me in Europe, and besides that, I have no European experience."

Laila took Kurt's hand. Her exasperation had faded. He looked tired and older than his age. She could feel his disappointment. It was in his blue eyes. He couldn't hide from her. The promotion he'd thought he deserved had slipped through his fingers once again. He knew the company would never recognise his hard work.

"When do we leave? You know I'll follow you to the ends of the earth, Kurt," Laila joked, trying to make light of the move. She kissed him gently on the cheek. It was packing time again.

Zambia couldn't be that bad, even if she knew from past conversations that the Lusaka hotel was an old lady. It badly needed a face-lift—more like full reconstructive surgery—and business was far from booming.

Surely, it couldn't compare to what Kurt found on arrival in Lagos. There had been no sight of a toilet on the construction site; workers, including the previous general manager, civil engineer and project manager, were relieving themselves in the bushes!

How had the owner envisaged the opening in six months' time?

Furniture and fittings had been ordered four years earlier only to rot in storage. It was an incredible feat on Kurt's part that the hotel had opened its doors a year later. After six years of construction work, the owner finally had an operating hotel.

Kurt had interviewed and employed not only the fifteen expatriates from executive chef, housekeeper and human resources manager to his personal assistant but the other three hundred employees. He had sifted through hundreds of resumes, and head-hunters became friends, with the amount of time he held discussions with them.

Toilets and bathtubs had been tested for leakages in all three hundred and sixty rooms, as had lifts and water sprinklers in case of fire. Food items on all five outlet menus had been tasted and decided upon. Staff were trained, and uniforms argued about for design and authenticity with the executive housekeeper. Guests had to see a touch of West Africa from the moment they were greeted, Kurt argued. Finally, they had settled on a compromise—a western uniform with touches of African colour, either in an elaborate headscarf for front office staff or trimmings for housekeeping and food and beverage employees.

Bathroom amenities had been sniffed at and compared, Laila trying out body lotions, bubble bath and shampoo from Elemis, L'Occitane, Zegna, Fragonard and other brands. She'd also been a willing guinea pig for potential masseuses for the spa. Thai, hot stone, Swedish, Balinese, aromatherapy, relaxing and head massages were complimentary stress busters.

"Lie with your face down and cover yourself with the towel." Whether she was vacationing in Mauritius or living in Egypt, it was standard. Only a contortionist could carry out such a feat. Did massage therapists the world over realise the folly of the statement?

Every nitty-gritty detail had been seen too. The flagship hotel Kurt was managing had finally opened its doors. The incoming general manager had been promoted to regional director! All's fair in love and war.

When no candidate had been found to replace Kurt's predecessor after the owner tired of no progress on his property in Lagos, the CEO had called Kurt. What he lacked in stature, the CEO made up in ego. The men were as different as chalk and cheese.

"We require a general manager for Lagos, Kurt. Are you interested? The salary is forty percent more than what you're getting, plus hardship allowance."

"I'll have to speak with my wife. I'll let you know, Edward." Kurt had been enthusiastic about the new venture. Little did he know of the construction shambles that he would encounter.

When Kurt had phoned back two days later with his agreement, the conversation had been brief.

"The new contract will be sent to you shortly. You'll start in six weeks. Just so we are clear, you're on your own over there," Edward stated dryly.

"On my own? What do you mean?" Kurt was baffled. The years they had spent together in university had led them down different paths. Edward knew how to polish shoes.

"I can't stand the owner. Expect no support from me. Your job is to get the hotel open and running."

The dialling tone rang loud in Kurt's ear. True to his word, Edward had kept to his side of the bargain, and Kurt had been thrown into the lion's den.

There were no phone calls or emails on how work was progressing. No words of encouragement when the situation quickly evolved and progress was achieved in leaps and bounds.

"How come your bosses never offer you destinations in the French Riviera, Los Angeles, Paris, London, Seychelles or Vietnam?" Laila was exasperated by the unfairness of it all.

"Laila, they could offer Damascus, Tripoli, Baghdad, Venezuela or Aden. We're lucky."

Laila made a face behind Kurt's back. His loyalty was mind-boggling. She wanted to take the halo round his head and strangle him with it.

It was outrageous how top bosses always wanted more. More profit, more occupancy, more staff satisfaction. Always more. It was funny how double standards worked with some and a blind eye was turned with others. Laila knew it was pointless arguing with Kurt.

"When do you start?"

"In two weeks. They need someone immediately." Kurt's broad shoulders stooped.

They want you out of the way, but Laila didn't say it. Promotion once again for the incoming blue-eyed guy!

"Two weeks? They're in a hurry?"

Kurt shrugged. Laila could see that he didn't want to elaborate.

Instead, she said, "The suitcases will be packed and we're ready to go."

It had been years since Laila had stopped travelling with cargo. Picture frames, furniture—including a magnificent mahogany Steinway piano with ivory keys that she had bought at a bargain—ornaments, kitchen equipment, tennis racquets and golf clubs had been left behind in the house in France. With the girls in England, all she and Kurt needed were clothes.

Only last week she had dismissed the maid. She had come home from the Spar Supermarket to find Happiness in her silk trousers and hand-knitted cashmere top. Guilelessly, she'd had the audacity to open the door in Laila's clothes! Happiness had helped herself to makeup from the dressing table to doll up her face and had even painted her finger- and toenails, all of which had horrified Laila. How often did she do this? She had even taken the liberty of wearing Laila's lacy bra.

Meticulous as always, Laila had discarded all lingerie and makeup. All clothes were dispatched for dry-cleaning.

"You're like my sister-o," Happiness had begged. "Please don't fire me now, Ma."

"Do you use your sister's things without permission-o?" Laila demanded, livid.

Flour, sugar or rice had disappeared on a weekly basis and she had turned a blind eye. Torches, lamps and mobile phones for Happiness and her entire family had been charged every day under the guest room bed. A relative picked up charged items at lunchtime and replaced them with a new batch. Electricity cuts were daily and generators were owned by the privileged few. But using her clothes and cosmetics was taking it too far.

"Where will I go now-o, Ma?"

"You should have thought about that before, Happiness."

More reason why Laila preferred living in the hotel. Housekeeping had little chance of parading in her clothes or eating her food. Did Happiness have aspirations of being Jennifer Lopez in *Maid in Manhattan*!

It was time to move, to leave the hustle and bustle of Lagos.

Rats scuttling on supermarket shelves and fridges had taken a lot of getting used to. The shriek Laila had let out the first time had brought the supermarket to a standstill! The constant need to be on guard, whether against car-jacking, kidnapping or scams—from winning millions in the lottery to witchcraft—was giving Laila an ulcer as big as a crater. Corruption was rife. Everyone expected something in return, from the vegetable seller in the kiosk whose scale was set at half a kilo extra to the managing director of the petroleum company.

Centre of Excellence embossed on all licence plates was an exaggeration!

***

They went from one extreme to another.

Kenneth Kaunda Airport was small and doll-like in comparison to Mohammed Murtala International Airport. It was clean. That perked up Laila's spirits. A welcome change from Lagos!

Immediately it dawned on Laila that Zambians preferred the slow lane in life. Thunderstorms and heavy rain would find them walking calmly without an umbrella, unperturbed. Nigerians would scuttle for shelter at the sign of drizzle! Afraid to ruin expensive handbags, wigs, shoes and outfits.

The fast pace of Lagos was exchanged for a slower pace. While other African countries were developing and booming with skyscrapers and infrastructure, Lusaka was taking off with escalators. Riding one was a family outing. Groups of children ran up, then down, giggling, having a ball. Parents watched in fascination, taking photo after photo. *Mzungus* sighed loudly in frustration, having to wait on an escalator with heaving food trolleys for an uncrowded ride.

The white Zambians were stuck in the colonial era, with their 'servants' wearing white gloves and white uniforms with gold buttons. Laila felt like she had stepped into a scene of *Out of Africa* and Meryl Streep and Robert Redford would appear at a lunch or dinner. Time seemed to have stood still since David Livingston arrived in landlocked Zambia.

In Lagos, there had been polo tournaments and Nollywood parties where Veuve Cliquot champagne or Johnnie Walker Blue, Gold or Green Label was the only alcohol served. Cigars and fine cognac jazz bars were available from Victoria Island to Lekki. Kelly Rowland, Beyoncé, Tinie Tempah and Usher concerts were monthly affairs. Sunday brunches in top hotels started with pink champagne, caviar and oysters. An entrance fee of five hundred dollars was paid as easily as a tip in exclusive nightclubs.

Smart casual in Zambia meant flip-flops and shorts! From the swanky affairs in the Middle East to the OTT ones in Lagos, Lusaka was on a different latitude.

Laila loved Zambia. She felt safe walking the open markets, haggling for curios, African fabric and fruits and vegetables. Indeed, life was slow-paced, but that only added to its charm. Skyscrapers, technology and swanky restaurants could be found anywhere.

The local people were warm, humble and friendly. They certainly didn't know the meaning of pretension. Even the expat community were welcoming and didn't pry as much or pass condescending remarks as they had done in other countries.

She was happy and so was Kurt. The coffee mornings and ladies' lunches had been put on the back-burner. Laila was bored of entertaining; she wanted something more. Laila never had the urge to grill people at functions about social positions or their children's achievements.

"Where're you from?" How many times had Laila answered this question? Yet she had never felt the need to pose it to anyone. Did it matter where you came from?

"How old are your children?" The actual question was how old was she, but they didn't dare ask that outright!

It was an artificial life, this glamorous one she'd lived for so many years, where pretension was the cherry on the cake and rubbing shoulders with people who were more fake than the Louis Vuitton bags in a Hong Kong market was the norm. She was tired of the air kisses, plastic smiles and nonchalance. She was tired of the Joneses keeping up with the Kamaus and Duponts.

Kurt worked extra hard in Lusaka. The hotel had been left to deteriorate to an almost no-star hotel. He tried to boost the flagging morale of the employees and bring back five-star standards in the rooms and restaurants.

"I salute Mr Petticoat for giving us a salary increment," Agnes, the room attendant, told Laila. "No one thought about us in the last five years."

"Don't tell me, Agnes, you must tell him yourself. He'll be pleased."

Staff were motivated and profits were on the rise. Businessmen were returning. There was no comparing an ageing hotel of over fifty years to the modern, fashionable designer brands found in

Singapore, Abu Dhabi or Kuala Lumpur, but it was once again the hotel to be seen at in the city.

An idea was forming in Laila's head. She needed to take life into her own hands. It was time she found her wings. Lakshmi would have wanted her to soar, and Laila knew that she would.

***

Laila sat at the small corner table at La Dolce Vita. It was a sunny day in London, a beautiful change from the fine drizzle and damp of the day before. It was mid-May, warm enough to do without a jacket.

People were bustling on their way to or from lunch. Dapper men in dark suits and elegantly dressed ladies tottering in skyscraper heels, perfectly made up.

Laila glanced at her Baume and Mercier wristwatch. It had been a present from Kurt years ago. The Roman numerals caught the sunlight streaming through the window.

She was nervous. How was she to broach the subject of their father to the girls? She had discussed it with Kurt, and he had wanted her to tell their daughters before he spoke to them. Was he embarrassed? Guilty? Ashamed? They had waited long enough.

It was time.

Laila had struggled with Kurt's homosexuality for a long time. Gradually, she had come to accept it and accept Kurt for the man he was. He had been her husband. He was her friend now. They were strong together. Laila could count on Kurt and he on her. She never asked if he had someone in his life. She didn't think so, unless he was extremely discreet. He had kept to his side of the bargain all those years ago, not to bring his personal life into their home.

"Hello, Mama." Lili enveloped Laila in a bear hug. "Sorry I'm late. Have you been waiting long?"

Laila hugged her daughter tight. She was breathtakingly beautiful. A confident, bubbly twenty-two year old, freshly graduated.

"Lalita isn't with you?"

"She got a call from one of her endless friends. Social networking, as usual." Lili laughed. "She's one person who could never live without her mobile."

Lalita breezed into the café, a wide grin on her oval face. She was tall and thin. Just as beautiful as her sister. Looking at them, no one would think they had Indian blood running through their veins.

"Maman!" Lalita squealed for the entire restaurant to hear.

The conversation rotated around their life in London, art and history studies at university for Lalita and a job at a trendy fashion magazine for Lili.

"How is Lusaka? Do you like it?" Lalita held her mother's hand while she forked some lettuce leaves in her mouth.

"Lusaka is the same. Slow, but the people are wonderful and we have a full social calendar. Your father knows every ambassador, minister and managing director. Even the president calls him by his first name when he comes to the hotel, which is often!"

"Are you happy?" Lili looked at her mother candidly.

Laila took a few seconds to reply. "Yes, I am. Very happy." She put her fork down, then continued, "I need to tell you girls something that's weighed heavy on my heart for several years."

She paused, trying to get the words right. They were adults, better able to understand sexual orientation.

"Your father is gay," Laila said the sentence slowly but firmly, looking both her daughters in the eye. The silence was deafening, but the shock that Laila had braced herself for didn't materialise. "Did you hear me?"

"We heard, Ma. We know," Lalita answered. She still held Laila's hand, only tighter now.

"You know? How long have you girls known? Why haven't you said anything? I've been agonising over this moment for years and years."

"We suspected a few years ago. We noticed while growing up that the kissing and cuddling had come to an end."

Lili took Laila's other hand. "We knew it had to do with the time in Oman when you were sad for months and months. When you barely spoke. When Papa walked around like a zombie." She kissed the tips of Laila's fingers.

The three women sat in silence for a long while. Tears from Laila's eyes fell onto the white tablecloth. She released her hands from Lili and Lalita's grasp to brush away her tears.

"We didn't want you to worry about us and our feelings for Papa." Lili swallowed the lump. Her voice was breaking. "We just didn't want the two of you to be sad."

"Nothing will change the love we have for you or for Papa. Nothing!" Lalita said vehemently, shaking her perfectly cut bob.

Relief swept over Laila like a tidal wave. No more secrets. Her daughters were doing her proud.

They weren't bitter, angry or upset. When had they grown up?

Still, Kurt would have to tell them. He owed them that much. He needed to look them in the eye, tell them how much he loved them.

"I have something else to tell you, as you took away the thunder from my headliner," Laila said, smiling.

"What? More?" Lili asked, hitting her forehead in an exaggerated fashion. "There's only so much that we can take, right Lali?" She winked at her sister.

"It's nothing ground-shattering." Laila paused. "I've supported both of you and your father all these years. I need time for me. I've decided to go to Rwanda to help women and young children. It's something I'll enjoy. It will be a change from the luxurious but often pretentious life I've led. I want to be appreciated and to appreciate others for what they are. I want to find my place. I'd like to make a difference, even if it's only a small difference in someone else's life. I'd like to make others happy. I think I can in this totally different environment. I know it won't be easy, as I've grown used to a certain lifestyle, but I'd really like to give it a go." Laila's hazel eyes shone as she swallowed the lump in her throat.

The three of them were crying.

"Do you understand?"

"Ma, we understand perfectly," Lalita said softly. "We can't be selfish. If that's what you want, if it will make you happy, then you deserve it. You've sacrificed so much for us; we can't ask for anything more."

"Except for your happiness," Lili added, barely raising a perfectly arched eyebrow.

Laila was bursting with joy. Her precious daughters understood.

"I'll tell your father that I've spoken to you girls. Expect a call from him. He has his own explaining to do."

The girls smiled at Laila.

"Your generation are more open-minded in a fast-evolving world," she said. "It's good. Times are changing. We—I have changed too. I wish I had told your grandma. I think she would have understood, but I was too afraid of her reaction, of her judgement perhaps. Most of all I didn't want her to stop loving your father."

"Nan understands," Lili said quietly. "She loved Pa unconditionally."

"When do you leave?" Lalita asked, changing the subject. She seemed to sense the sadness, and how much her mother missed her grandmother.

"Next month. I'm waiting for my paperwork to come through. Your father will continue working in Lusaka. I'm so excited about this new and different adventure in my life."

***

November 2013

Glory was waiting at the gate. The stubs she had for arms were wide open. Instead of a nose, she had a gaping hole. Her skin was pulled tight over her cheekbones. Leprosy had eaten through her flesh many years ago but not through her heart. No disease could keep at bay the warmth and love that Glory exuded. She was a ray of sunshine.

"Mama Laila, *karibu sana.* Welcome. Welcome. Was the safari good? Are you not too tired? Let me take your suitcase. Did you find Theodore at the airport? I told that lazy boy to be sure to pick you up on time. Your *sanduku* is heavy. What have you put in it? I have got you many kitenge for comfortable dresses. How is your family? Your daughters are good? And the bwana good also?" Once Glory got talking, there was no stopping her.

Laila smiled and nodded. This was her third trip to the country. The first two had been short stays to familiarise herself with the project, process a resident visa and meet various NGOs. This time, she would be staying for much longer.

She stared at the elaborately painted sign above the gate. It was colourful and welcoming, with a border of flowers and ethnic patterns.

Bahati shelter for women and children

This was her new home. *Bahati*, luck in Swahili.

The shelter would take in women who had suffered violence in their household, rape victims, widows or women who had nowhere to go, along with their children. Orphans and abandoned children were welcomed into Laila's new haven. They would find peace, protection and love.

Before she could catch her breath, she was surrounded by children of all ages. "Mama Laila, Mama Laila!" The older ones tried to grab her hand or some part of her khaki trousers while they balanced babies on their tiny hips. Mama sounded comforting compared to ma'am, which hotel staff had addressed her by for over twenty years. There was a time when that had made her feel like the queen.

She had come a long way.

"*Watotos! Watotos! Wacha mama* Laila." Glory shooed the children away.

Laila put an arm around her shoulder, stopping her. "Glory, leave them be. I'm home now. This is what I came here for."

"But Mama Laila, you're tired."

"No, Glory, I'm not that tired." Laila picked up the chubby child next to her.

The child's nose was running, but her smile would melt ice in the North Pole. She cradled Laila's face in her tiny hands, feeling every contour like a blind person. Her charcoal eyes bore into Laila's. Finally, she completed her inspection. Seemly satisfied, she covered Laila's face in kisses. Laila hugged the child to her. A few years ago, her running nose and dusty limbs would have had her running for the nearest tap.

When was the last time she felt such joy? She had changed in more ways than she could imagine. Not only in the material sense, trading in her Sergio Rossi heels for Bata plimsolls. It was for the better, Laila was sure of that. She would find satisfaction here. She would be welcomed and loved. She would fit in.

"Chaka here approves of you. She will not let go of you. She will be your tail for the rest of your days here at Bahati." Glory meant her statement as ominous.

"Oh, Glory, you can't know how happy I am to be here." On impulse, Laila kissed Glory loudly on her cheeks. "Together we will make Bahati the most talked about place in the whole of Rwanda. With help from donations from the outside world, we'll slowly build a school, bring running water and educate both mothers and their children so they can better their lives."

"I know, Mama Laila. God is good."

CHAPTER 11

"THIS IS ME"

February 2015

Guilt swaddled Laila like a gauze bandage. She hadn't thought of her mother in a week. A whole week. How could Lakshmi not have crossed her mind? In the years since Lakshmi's death, she had thought about her religiously several times a day. She spoke to her in the morning, asked for advice when she was at a crossroads, talked to her again in the evening, prayed for her soul, cooked meals the way she had taught her and played her favourite songs. She was like an invisible shadow by Laila's side each day, nudging her along.

"I'm sorry, Ma," Laila whispered. "I've not forgotten you. I'll never forget you."

There were days after Lakshmi's death when Laila had thought she would never get over her grief. Her mountain had crumbled, and she was grappling in the rubble, struggling to find her mother in the debris. Her head was held underwater, and grief was rushing out of her ears and eyes. Every pore in her body had oozed grief. She would surface spluttering, gasping for breath. The void Lakshmi had left was too deep to fill. Her absence was felt like a stitch in the side: nagging, all-encompassing, frustrating and painful.

Laila couldn't bring herself to ask Amit how he felt, knowing he must be drowning in his own ocean. It was the Indian way. A father merited respect and was only spoken to when absolutely necessary. Even now, at fifty-eight years of age, she couldn't cross that barrier, break down the wall.

She remembered how Aunt Deepa had insisted that Lakshmi shouldn't be cremated.

"It's not in our religion. She should be buried like a good Catholic."

Laila had glared at Deepa. "My mother insisted on being cremated. Those were her wishes, and *I* will abide by them. If you're not comfortable, then please don't attend the cremation."

Yes, cremation wasn't part of the Catholic religion but neither was unkindness, meanness nor hatred, yet it never stopped anyone. Why was religion wielded like a sword? To keep believers from straying? Was the fear of God's wrath meant to keep the faithful in check? Did it?

***

October 1975

"Why are you crying, Mummy?"

Laila was almost sixteen. She hated to see her mother cry. Lakshmi's tears did something to her heart. She felt like her body was going through a mincer, squeezing out every drop of blood.

"Today is sixteen years since my mother passed away." Lakshmi looked forlorn. She wiped her tears on the sleeve of her chunky black sweater and sniffed loudly. "I miss her so much."

"Sixteen years! Such a long time ago! Why are you still crying?" The outspoken teenager hadn't known how to deal with the situation. Looking back, her words were cruel. Laila knew she had been brutally brusque with her mother.

"Laila, my child, it doesn't matter whether it's sixteen or sixty years, I still miss her. One day you'll go through the same feeling. You know, she died two months before you were born." Lakshmi took Laila's face in her hands and smiled sadly. "How I wish you could have met your grandmother. You're exactly like her."

"Good. Then she wouldn't want you to cry after so many years."

"Will it make you happy if I stop?"

"Yes!"

"You're a funny girl. There are days when you dislike me, then, like today, you can't bear to see me cry." Lakshmi smiled through her tears. Her honey-coloured eyes could melt Laila's heart. Her mother was astute.

The previous few years had been topsy-turvy for Laila. Being a teenager was difficult. Most days she'd loved Lakshmi with all her heart, but other days she wanted to scream and throw something at her. When she wished that she had anyone else as a mother, Lakshmi never berated her. She would sit Laila down and ask her quietly what was wrong.

"I'm your mother, Laila my child. You can talk to me about anything."

On Laila's good days, which weren't many, she didn't mind being called 'my child', but on a stroppy day, it irritated her. She wasn't a child any longer.

Lakshmi had bought her a book titled *A Girl Grows Up*. Laila had finished reading it in a day.

She had loved it. The book had explained what was going on in her body, the changes, what she should expect, how to deal with girl and boy friends, parents and siblings. Lakshmi didn't know that Laila slept with the book under her pillow. She had wanted to share this wonderful book with her friends in school, especially Urvashi, but had thought better of it. No book would help Urvashi's moodiness. Laila guarded it possessively. It was her go-to reference book, her teenage encyclopaedia. Every night, she re-read a chapter before tucking it under her pillow.

Laila had treasured the book for years. When it mysteriously disappeared, she turned her tiny pink bedroom inside out in search of it. She wanted to hand it down to her own children when she married.

Her teenage crisis had vanished like the book. She was a young bride moving into the hotel world with her knight in shining armour.

After Lili's birth, Laila's love for Lakshmi had grown and grown. She had told Lakshmi that she would never fight with her ever again as she cradled the tiny, hour-old bundle.

"If you don't quarrel with me, our lives will be dull and pointless, my child. Being a mother is the most difficult job in the world. But it's also beautiful and rewarding." Lakshmi had let out one of her boisterous laughs. "My baby doll has her own baby doll."

Their fights had grown fewer and fewer. Laila had left her job when Lalita was born. She couldn't cope with the terror that Lalita was. The child never slept. Lakshmi's presence in the hotel apartment was a godsend. From 7:00 a.m. to 5:00 p.m., her mother did whatever she could to lighten Laila's workload. Laila could never thank her enough. She was eternally grateful.

***

February 2015

In her little room in Rwanda, Laila held the frayed piece of paper in her hands. It had been read and re-read a thousand times over the years. The folds in the paper were thin and crumply, and the ink had faded in many parts. It was Laila's sixteenth birthday present from Lakshmi.

At the time, Laila had been annoyed with her mother. What kind of present was this? What mother gave her daughter a poem? She had cried, pleaded and begged for the fashionable shoes in the Bata shop for weeks.

"You have your whole life, my child, to wear high heels. There's a time for everything."

Laila had stormed out of the room, yelling how much she hated her.

"I wish I was dead!"

Lakshmi had let her sulk in her room for a couple of days. Eventually, Laila made do with the ugly flat shoes. Either she wore them or went barefoot!

Life had thrown Laila many curveballs. She had ducked some and caught some over the years. She wasn't rich in friendships. They had eluded her—or had she eluded them, with her desperate need for privacy?

She had few friends.

Divya, who she had met in Saudi Arabia. Even though they were not in touch with each other on a daily or even monthly basis, they knew they had each other. The calls at Christmas and on their birthdays were long and nostalgic. Laila knew she only had to pick up the phone to find a true friend at the other end.

Karina was a friend she thought of often, especially at Roland-Garros season, when her life had tumbled out of control. Laila hoped with social media she would find her again one day but so far had come up against a blank wall.

Narmin and Julia would hold a special place in her heart. The three of them had gone through a rollercoaster period in Congo. They kept in touch on a regular basis. There was a promise of a visit to Rwanda in the pipeline.

Her perfect marriage had crumbled before her eyes with Kurt's betrayal with another man. She had thought she would die of a broken heart. She hadn't. They had come to a compromise. With time, the hurt had faded to leave in its place a beautiful, firm friendship with a man she would always love, the father of her two beautiful daughters.

The divorce papers had been signed just a few weeks ago. Laila had cried for a long time. The relationship they had kept up for appearances and for their daughters had come to an end.

They were both free.

Kurt was happy. He had spoken to his daughters, and they understood and loved him. That was important for him. For all of them as a family. Laila knew there was no one special in his life, as yet. She wished him well, knowing they would be there for each other.

Laila read the words of the poem by Rudyard Kipling, written in her mother's beautiful handwriting. Lakshmi had changed the last line.

If you can keep your head when all about you
Are losing theirs and blaming it on you;
If you can trust yourself when all men doubt you,
But make allowance for their doubting too;
If you can wait and not be tired by waiting,
Or being lied about, don't deal in lies,
Or being hated, don't give way to hating,
And yet don't look too good, nor talk too wise:

If you can dream—and not make dreams your master;
If you can think—and not make thoughts your aim;
If you can meet with Triumph and Disaster
And treat those two impostors just the same;
If you can bear to hear the truth you've spoken
Twisted by knaves to make a trap for fools,
Or watch the things you gave your life to, broken,
And stoop and build 'em up with worn-out tools:

If you can make one heap of all your winnings
And risk it on one turn of pitch-and-toss,
And lose, and start again at your beginnings
And never breathe a word about your loss;
If you can force your heart and nerve and sinew
To serve your turn long after they are gone,
And so hold on when there is nothing in you
Except the Will which says to them: "Hold on!"

If you can talk with crowds and keep your virtue,
Or walk with Kings—nor lose the common touch;
If neither foes nor loving friends can hurt you,
If all men count with you, but none too much;
If you can fill the unforgiving minute
With sixty seconds' worth of distance run
Yours is the Earth and everything that's in it,
And—which is more—you'll be a Woman, my child!

Laila wiped her eyes on the sleeve of the worn-out sweater. She was lucky to have had such a wise, wonderful woman for her mother. The poem had taken her through the hills and vales of her life. She knew it by heart but held on to the piece of paper preciously. Of all the presents Laila had received, this one was priceless.

"Thank you, my Mummy. I have so much to thank you for," she whispered.

Lakshmi had given her wings. Other people may have tried to clip them, but Laila knew she would soar always, the way Lakshmi wanted her to.

Laila looked at the photo of Lakshmi. "Now I know how you felt all those years ago. You mourned your own mother for years, the way I mourn you now. The path ahead I'll have to walk alone. I'll have to grapple in the dark at times without your advice or wisdom, but I know that I can climb mountains and swim the choppiest oceans. After all, you raised me up."

In the last couple of months, Laila's life had changed tremendously. She lived in a sparse room. A bed and a small table were the only furniture. An empty bottle of Fanta held two fragrant roses. The wall opposite her bed was wallpapered with photographs of Lili and Lalita. Some of Kurt; he had been a big part of her life. An old photo of a young Lakshmi, with a big smile and twinkling eyes, before the disease had ravaged her. A few photos of Amit, who seemed to have shrunk with age. A family photo of Tamer, Kara and the boys. Scenery she had loved in the places she had lived.

Happy memories.

The room was draped in sunlight from the large window that gave a magnificent view of acacia trees and rolling green hills in the distance. The verdant land took her breath away every morning. Sometimes, on a still day, the roar of gorillas in the forest could be heard faintly. The heavy perfume of the rows of rose bushes wafted into the room. Glory had insisted on planting them. Red for love, red for blood, she had said.

The radio was tuned to BBC Radio 2. The reception was never very clear, but through the crackle and static, Laila listened to her foreign friends. Chris Evans no longer did the breakfast show. He had been replaced by Zoe Ball, and Lynn Bowles had moved to her native Scotland. Ken Bruce continued his banter with Richie Anderson, and Laila looked forward to Pop Master every weekday at 9:30 a.m. She was kept up-to-date with traffic info on Spaghetti Junction or the M6 and train and tube services, delays and strike action. Graham Norton had stepped down from his Saturday morning show. Laila missed his cheekiness and sense of humour.

The new and old presenters followed Laila in her routine, be it weeding the immaculate garden or planting tomatoes, leeks, potatoes, courgettes, aubergines or rows of fragrant herbs. They were the background noise while she read or pored over the accounts. She listened with one ear while she taught the children, and over their boisterous playing while the sun set in the evenings. This was the one link she still retained to her old world, the glamourous one she had lived in for years.

"What joke did Bwana Ken Bruce tell you today, Mama Laila? How is Bwana Ken Bruce this fine morning? What song will Bwana Ken Bruce play to make you tap your feet?"

Laila loved the way Glory called Ken Bruce "Mister". The days they worked together, Glory noticed how Laila guffawed, smirked or just smiled while listening to the radio.

"I don't understand the bwana's jokes."

"You have to have lived in Europe, Glory, to understand the jokes."

Happiness flowed through Laila. A few years ago she would never have dreamed of living life in a remote village in Rwanda. She coped now with water shortages and minimal electricity. When was the last time she'd had a body massage? The shoulder rubs Glory gave her some evenings with the stub of her arms around the open-air fire were better than many massages at deluxe spas she had frequented.

The gastronomic meals and Michelin-star dinners she had enjoyed were replaced by boiled rice and goat meat stews flavoured with basil or rosemary or laurel. Beef was a luxury. The meals were hearty and delicious in comparison to immaculately plated portions. Vegetables grew in abundance and were fresh and tasty, unlike the supermarket ones. Tennis and golf were exchanged for long walks in the forests with the children singing loudly in delight. Sunsets and moonrises were gazed at in awe in the company of people who loved her and whom she loved. Even the thunderstorms were welcomed. Water was life.

The hectic, bustling world of luxurious lobbies and air-conditioned rooms with white linen and fluffy towels couldn't compare to what she had gained in the little things in life.

There was no race here for the American National Day cocktail party or dinner at the British high commissioner's residence. Laila never had to ask herself what she should wear or say she didn't have anything to wear. She had become adept at wrapping the kitenge around her waist. A headscarf knotted neatly round her greying hair was a staple fashion accessory. She no longer needed to dye her roots glossy mahogany every four weeks. There were no women vying for her attention because she was the wife of the general manager of the five-star hotel in town. The borrowed title of "wife of the general manager" didn't exist here.

The women who vied for her attention were Glory, for the running of the accounts, and Margi, for the housekeeping. Gertrude, for the studies of the twenty-eight children who needed exercise and textbooks, and the acute lack of stationery.

The widows came to discuss the profit of their crops or the progress of their children in school. How to rid their plantations of the sparrows that ate their lettuces, and whose scarecrow was more innovative.

"I got twenty shillings more than last week for my potatoes, Mama Laila," Anna said, proudly.

"I got twenty-five for the green beans. Mr Kalinga said I could pick the avocadoes from his tree whenever I want as he doesn't eat them. I sell them for five shillings each." Jacintha wasn't to be outdone.

Those who didn't have green fingers made beautiful handbags and slippers with remnant pieces of kitenge, or earrings and bracelets. Others made beautiful, beaded placemats, coasters and tea-light holders.

Laila had managed to get the owner of the boutique in the luxurious five-star hotel to display the wares. Business was booming. Recently they had begun to receive personalised orders from expat ladies.

There were no questions asked. Where did she come from? What did she do before? What did her husband do? Was she friends with the Spanish, English or Japanese ambassador's wife? How big was the hotel apartment? How much help did she have? What were the perks?

Here, she was an enthusiastic volunteer who had adapted well in Rwanda.

No rain was a problem; electricity rationing was a problem; not enough donations for the mending of a roof or a generator was a problem. But these were small problems. There were no problems of skin colour here, nor position nor wealth nor education nor jealousy.

Everyone was equal. Everyone was happy.

Laila had finally found her place in life.

AUTHOR PROFILE

June's first passion is music, followed very closely by books—the two things she cannot live without. Whipping up cakes for family and friends is another way for her to unwind, and eavesdropping in restaurants and public venues is an obsession she cannot wean herself off!

***

WHAT DID YOU THINK OF YOU RAISED ME UP?

A big thank you for purchasing this book. It means a lot that you chose this book specifically from such a wide range on offer. I do hope you enjoyed it.

Book reviews are incredibly important for an author. All feedback helps them improve their writing for future projects and for developing this edition. If you are able to spare a few minutes to post a review on Amazon, that would be much appreciated.

PUBLISHER INFORMATION

Rowanvale Books provides publishing services to independent authors, writers and poets all over the globe. We deliver a personal, honest and efficient service that allows authors to see their work published, while remaining in control of the process and retaining their creativity. By making publishing services available to authors in a cost-effective and ethical way, we at Rowanvale Books hope to ensure that the local, national and international community benefits from a steady stream of good quality literature.

For more information about us, our authors or our publications, please get in touch.

www.rowanvalebooks.com
info@rowanvalebooks.com

Printed in Great Britain
by Amazon

84364297R00149